Intersections

Intersections

A Reading of Sade with
Bataille, Blanchot, and
Klossowski

Jane Gallop

UNIVERSITY OF NEBRASKA PRESS
Lincoln and London

Library of Congress Cataloging in Publication Data

Gallop, Jane, 1952–
   Intersections, a reading of Sade with Bataille, Blanchot, and
Klossowski.

   Includes index.
   1. Sade, Donatien Alphonse Francois, comte, called Marquis de,
1704–1814—Criticism and interpretation.   2. Bataille, Georges,
1897–1962—Knowledge—Literature.   3. Blanchot, Maurice—Knowledge—Literature.   4. Klossowski,   Pierre—Knowledge—
Literature.   I. Title.
PQ2063.S3G35   843'.6   80–23117
ISBN 0–8032–2110–X

For Alex, Jeffrey, Richard, and Neil

Contents

Introduction

THIS book focuses on the fiction of the Marquis de Sade through the filter of three readers of Sade, themselves important literary figures of postwar France: Georges Bataille, Maurice Blanchot, and Pierre Klossowski. These three writers have been influential in shaping a contemporary reading of Sade. Thus, rather than implicitly assume their influence and work blindly with or against it, we will examine instead the points of intersection of the four bodies of writing marked Sade, Bataille, Blanchot, and Klossowski. The present study then has two principal aims: (1) to say something new about what is at work in Sade's books and (2) to ascertain certain directions and peculiarities in the discourses of these three significant contributors to contemporary French thought.

This choice of an intertextual reading (a reading that does not respect textual

frontiers) is determined by the tradition, doubtless a
recent one, which assumes that a literary work is not
a closed unity reflecting the integrity either of the
person who creates it or of the person who beholds
it. The tradition can be termed—very loosely—structuralism, and its usual strategy has been to show how
the individual unit (whether word, ego, text, reader,
or writer) is, prior to its very constitution, already
alienated into a generalized system of exchange. This
orthodoxy will here be called "antihumanism" so as
to avoid the current problem of distinguishing between structuralism proper and poststructuralism.
Antihumanism can find a graphic parody of its characteristic gesture in the acts described in Sade's
books. Sadian libertines violate integrity and force
open closures. Just as antihumanist literary criticism
denies the sanctity of communication between writer
and reader by expropriating the individuality of both
into a determining network, so Sade's scenes frus-
trate "meaningful" sexual communion between two
partners relating to each other as "whole people" by
entangling the participants in complex meshes of
body parts and sexual acts.

   The pages that follow take their cue from this
parodic juxtaposition of Sadian text and antihumanist criticism. Scholarly critical discourse and graphic,
obscene language mingle in our attempt to execute
antihumanist literary criticism, not just upon Sade's
production, but as a repetition, an ever-reverberating
expansion of Sade's own writing. Sade alternately
presents pornographic scenes and philosophical harangues. The result of this mixture is that each undercuts the other. The brute impact of sex and
violence is softened, for they can be taken seriously,
can be studied and interpreted, as acting out certain

philosophical questions (for example: the reality of
the existence of others, the arbitrary nature of morality). Concurrently, philosophy's seriousness is tainted
through the exposure of the equivocal intersubjective
relations always underlying it.

The move to contaminate philosophy, whether
in Sade's mode of scandal and sensationalism or in
the current critical mode of carefully considered
questioning of philosophy's a priori ideology, is an
attack on the hierarchical distinction, underlying
Western metaphysics since Plato, between the ideal
(selfsame, replicable, worthy of philosophic discussion) and the material (messy, peculiar, obscene).
Modern continental philosophy, typified by a current
running through Friedrich Nietzsche, Martin Hei-
degger, and Jacques Derrida, strives continually to
undermine that entrenched hierarchy, to loosen its
hold. Antihumanist literary criticism leans on and
even participates in the "deconstruction" (the term
with which Derrida designates this philosophic gesture) of that segregation. This effort to mess up philosophy accounts for the great interest in Sade
evidenced in antihumanist circles (work on Sade by
Jacques Lacan, Michel Foucault, Roland Barthes,
Gilles Deleuze, Philippe Sollers, to name but a few of
the best known).

Tied up in the ideal / material hierarchy is the
sexist hierarchy, masculine / feminine. France has
produced a "deconstructive" feminism, daughter of
antihumanism. It is along these lines that the present
book is a feminist enterprise. As Sade stresses the
sexual underpinnings of the philosophical and the
political, as Sade violates certain sexual identities,
so our reading, a Sadian antihumanism, becomes
necessarily a feminist disturbance of the distinction

masculine / feminine and the correlative privilege of
the male, ideal sphere.

Sade displays another similarity to antihumanist
criticism. Throughout Sade's writing there recurs a
characteristic moment when activities outside a narration take up where activities within the narration
leave off: a moment that is possible because both
inside and outside are encompassed by a second-
level narration. This moment makes the activity of
storytelling rather equivocal, as if it were a seduction
of the listener who is drawn into the story by the
structure of the reading process. Antihumanist criticism questions the innocence of narration by exposing the violence done to the closed identities of
narrator and narratee through their alienation into
the textual network of the story.

Justine again and again tells her woeful tale only
to find her listener inspired to perpetrate crimes
upon her that resemble those she has just recounted.
In *120 Journées de Sodome*, every day the four principal characters listen to stories, choose victims, and
act out the passions they have just heard described.
The present book, in a similar gesture, tells the story
of a group of readers of Sade so as to imply that these
new characters take up where Sade's own characters
leave off. Thus, although my tale is restricted to a
very specific group of readers and their relation to a
particular corpus, because the moral of the story
bears upon the relation between the inside (characters) and the outside (readers) of that body of writing,
it may suggest something about reading in general,
or more specifically about perversion in writing
about reading, that is, in the realm of literary criticism.

Perversion must be defined as deviation from a norm, but Sade, according to Pierre Klossowski, thinks perversion to be already implicit in all the normal institutions of society. Sade's deviation is his explicitness: he creates a scandal by exposing what is universal, yet covert. Sade's gesture is not the controlled device of a reformer, not the tendentious exposé of a muckraker in the service of an imagined better world. There is no alternative presented to the evils uncovered. The perversity of this exposure is not justified by any basic humanist goal. As part of this unveiling, Sade breaks with the libertine literary tradition by opening up the *maison close* (brothel) and moving the action out into the world. Sade's characters are not outside society. They are judges, priests, prime ministers, doctors, and teachers gleaning perverted pleasures in the very pursuit of their professions, thereby affording Sade the opportunity for laying bare the libidinal interest underlying these serious, upright activities. I will extend the cast of characters to include writers and readers, literary critics.

The first of my four principal characters[1] is, of course, *Donatien Alphonse François, called Marquis, de Sade*, who spent twenty-seven of the seventy-four years of his life (1740–1814) incarcerated. He was removed from society on various specific charges, all of which, whether sexual crimes or the publication of improper books, can be grouped under the general charge of excessive activities lacking utilitarian value for society. Indeed, the condemnation of Sade as antisocial bridges gaping political differences since he was locked up by the *ancien régime*, the Reign of Terror, *and* the Empire. After his death his works were imprisoned in the *enfer* of the library, so that in the nineteenth century his audience was covert. However, in our century Sade has returned to circulation in society, thanks to the efforts of men such as Guillaume Apollinaire, Maurice Heine, and Gilbert Lély. Sade continues to meet with legal obstruction: the trial of the Editions Pauvert in the fifties resulted in a ban upon Sade's more obscene works. Yet, regardless of residual resistance, Sade is now widely read. He has his place within the anti-humanist literary community as the exemplary outcast. Current writing about Sade is frequent, with due mention always made of his exclusion from the literary canon.

Sade wrote long, long novels and one-page *historiettes* and, writing up until his death, tried his hand at most of the sizes and shapes in between. Not all of his works are obscene, but a good many are. Sade's biography includes some deviant sexual behavior (with erotic infliction of physical pain, but not murder), at least one grand passion (his sister-in-law), and at least one peaceful, comforting love (Marie-Constance Quesnet, who shared the last twenty years of his life, following him even into the asylum Charenton when he was confined there for immorality). Although both his detractors and his admirers have usually emphasized his monstrosity, this character is at times amiable and compassionate.

Sade is perhaps all the more frightening by being at once as monstrous as reputed and yet still very sympathetic. Others before have remarked upon the contrast between the cruel inhumanity found in his writings and the human emotion betrayed in many of Sade's real-life actions. Although it is neater thus to separate and stabilize the two poles, Sade's contradictions pervade both life and work. The writings in all their violence are also filled with tender sentiments and simple pleasures, just as the life with its many humane and socially responsible deeds is racked by perversion.

Sade functions as an object of fascination for the three other major characters:

Georges Bataille (1897–1962) is the most obvious descendant of Sade. Founder of the influential review *Critique*, novelist and essayist, Bataille, especially since his death, serves, like his hero Sade, as a popular focus for contemporary, antihumanist French thought. Bataille wrote "dirty books," and like Sade took very seriously the problem of eroticism and its eccentric yet powerful relation to human existence. Bataille was particularly preoccupied by the effort to expand the "human sciences" (economics, anthropology, sociology) so that they might more adequately confront the extravagant, irrational activities of both the sacred and the obscene domains. Today Bataille and Sade are often grouped together.[2]

The destiny of the character Bataille unfolds as the central irony of the present story. At the beginning Bataille is still alive, and is caught misreading Sade in a manner that would make the eighteenth-century author coincide with Bataille's own fantasies of sovereignty. Bataille's version has strongly influenced later readers and so his distortion of Sade into a "sovereign writer" has been accepted as an accurate image. The first chapter works to correct the confusion between Bataille's fantasies and the actual textual material by carefully examining Sade's text and extricating it from Bataille's constructions. Yet, after his death (after the first chapter), Bataille becomes more and more Sade until, by the end of this book, they are inextricably entangled.

Maurice Blanchot (born 1907) survives this story. He has written many works of fiction, none of which are obscene. On the contrary, Blanchot's texts are infuriatingly stingy with concrete details. The article under his name in the *Dictionnaire de Littérature Contemporaine* (Paris: Editions Universitaires, 1966) is the sole entry without an accompanying portrait of the author in question. Blanchot's critical writing is constantly concerned with the frightening and necessary alienation involved in writing. The enterprise of writing is, for Blanchot, the greatest risk, more dangerous than any "violent" activity, because it is the confrontation with loss of self, with a death that cannot even be recovered as the dramatic event of "one's own death."

Blanchot's move as a reader is always to find this featureless danger behind all the other contingent frights in any writer's production. The gesture proves truly persuasive, but frustratingly repetitive. In keeping with his emphasis upon the relatively comforting effects of specific violences as compared to this featureless violation of self, his fiction seems purified of the details that usually enable the reader to locate himself, to remember and classify the book by its individuality.

Blanchot's fascination with Sade, unlike Bataille's, does not bespeak a special inclination towards sex and violence. Rather, he must take on this body of writing despite its overabundance of details, so as to prove that beneath even these most forceful of graphic descriptions, the real violence, the real scandal, the real "action" is writing. Whereas Bataille fantasizes being Sade, the sovereign writer, Blanchot does not try to be Sade, but would unmask Sade as No One: that is, as an elusive lack of specific attributes, such as one that bears the name Maurice Blanchot.

Pierre Klossowski (born 1903) is the least known of the three contemporaries. There are two definite breaks in his life story: one around 1940 when he becomes a practicing Catholic; another in the fifties when he abjures the narrowness of his earlier work, moving beyond his Christianity to a more mainstream antihumanist, more Nietzschean position. Klossowski does write "dirty books." His novels are even similar to Sade's inasmuch as they juxtapose graphic sexual description and scholastic, theological debate. His interest in Sade spans the three periods of his career and can thus serve as a gauge in the examination of that disjointed history.

In 1947 Klossowski published *Sade mon prochain* (Paris: Seuil), which remains both the best-known book on Sade and the best-known book by Klossowski. A second edition of *Sade mon prochain* appeared in 1967, altered so it no longer promotes a Christian normalization of Sade's perversity. A comparison of the two editions affords us leverage for an understanding of Klossowski and helps explain the general effects of an antihumanist valorization of Sade.

In 1965 an issue of *Yale French Studies* (number 35) was devoted to Sade. *Tel Quel* published a Sade issue in 1967 (number 28). These two journals both present a text by Klossowski, the only author they share. Both of these texts appear in the second *Sade mon prochain*. The moment of the second version thus marks not only an efflorescence of interest in Sade, but also the possibility of a textual exchange, a flow between *Tel Quel* (as it was in 1967, more broadly representative of the mainstream of French antihumanism than it is today) and *Yale French Studies* (perhaps the best available gauge of the currents in American French studies).

The chapter on Klossowski, in a way, recapitulates and encompasses the entire book, for its story takes us from the period of the first *Sade mon prochain* up through the appearance of the second version. Thus the story ends over a decade before it is told. In the ensuing years, as a response to the writing of our three readers of Sade and many others like them in postwar France, a mature antihumanism (associated with names like Barthes, Derrida, Foucault, Lacan) came to great prominence and invaded American academia, where it already has a firm enough foothold to produce daughters and sons, working in and against their antihumanist heritage, who attempt books like this. . .

1 | Friendship—A Small Number of Exceptions: Bataille on Sade

> I abhor the entire universe
> except for the two friends you
> see here with me, and a few
> others: I sovereignly hate all
> the rest.
> —Saint-Fond in *Juliette* (8:209)[1]

A READER of Sade, exposed to the atmosphere of modern French thought, cannot escape being infected by Georges Bataille. Bataille's "sovereignty"—glorious expenditure as the possibility for a mingling of the most sacred and the unspeakably profane in their common transgression of the restricted economy of utility—is a "natural" accompaniment to Sade's outrageous excesses. Pierre Klossowski has been accused of actually meaning Bataille when he speaks of Sade,[2] but to have read Bataille may mean the impossibility of ever not reading Bataille when reading Sade.

The present book, in some first moment, attempts to wrap Bataille up in this first chapter and then leave him aside in order to go on to his friends Blanchot and Klossowski. Such would be the market economy (wrapped and labeled) of a book which aims to cover three readers of Sade.

In some first moment, the dismissal of Bataille appears exceedingly easy. His reading of Sade is the least complex, least equivocal of the three, and the distortions he must work in order to render Sade simple and pure are blatant.

Yet Bataille will not be left behind in this reading of Sade. The chapter on Blanchot must make space for Bataille, and the chapter on Klossowski is not only full of Bataille, but leads to a point hazardously close to Bataille's perspective (supposedly destroyed and abandoned in the first chapter). The danger in this final similarity to Bataille is heightened because the difference is simply between a masculine and a feminine mode, with the feminine an inconsistent simulation as well as a flighty derision of the masculine. To found an edifice upon the solidity of the distinction between masculine and feminine is a shaky project at best.

Roland Barthes writes: "Still much too much heroism in our idioms; in the best ones—I am thinking of Bataille's—, an erethism in certain expressions and finally a sort of *insidious heroism*. The pleasure of the text (the ecstasy of the text), on the contrary, is like a brusque effacement of warlike valour."[3] There is too much of the warrior who would give his life for a value in Bataille's sovereign man, too much of the solitary hyper-masculine hero in Bataille's Sade (at least in the properly Bataillian Sade, that which belongs to this chapter on Bataille). Here where he is catalogued and shelved, Bataille's Sade seems too upright and selfsame in his very extremes of outrage and self-destruction. As he seeps out, into chapters where it does not belong, he may shed his manly heroism and, lacking in all pride, remain, like a desperate woman clinging where she is not wanted.

That the scandalous Georges Bataille should read, write, and endorse the outrageous Marquis de Sade is all too fitting and proper. If, as Bataille claims, the normal man is necessary for Sade's effect to be outrage, then Bataille and Sade cancel each other out. Neither of the two provides resistance to the violence; so the aggression loses its thrust. The meeting of Bataille and Sade is too happy a conjunction not to throw askew Bataille's assertion that Sade poses an unassimilable threat to any solidarity between men.

Sade, according to Bataille, speaks "in the name of the silent life, in the name of a perfect, inevitably mute, solitude."[4] The paradoxical project thus ascribed to Sade is to speak the unspoken and the absolutely unspeakable. For Sade to accede to this perfect silence, he must commit himself to a self-destruction so complete that any trace of his ever having existed would be erased. Fully aware that Sade's concern for his books—in fact, the simple fact of writing—disallows Sade's speaking from the sovereign position ("in the name of the silent life"), Bataille locates the attitude of *insouciance* characteristic of sovereignty in Sade's last will and testament, where Bataille reads the following sentence: "Once the grave has been covered up, acorns will be sown upon it, so that . . . the traces of my tomb might disappear from the surface of the earth just as I flatter myself that my memory will disappear from men's memories."[5]

Bataille found this sentence in Apollinaire's *Oeuvre de Sade*,[6] where what is quoted here is the very end of the will and is followed immediately by

Sade's signature. However, this version of the paragraph is incomplete. Thus, the sentence where Bataille has Sade give proof of his "definitive silence," his sovereign lack of concern for his fellows, does not actually end so definitively: "the traces of my tomb might disappear from the surface of the earth just as I flatter myself that my memory will be erased from men's minds, except, nevertheless, for the small number of those who did try to love me up to the last moment."[7]

This exception of "the small number" absolutely undercuts Bataille's reading of the definitive silence. One cannot deny *autrui* (other people) and then make exceptions for a few close friends. Bataille's reading of Sade is not founded solely upon this one paragraph, so marginal to the marquis's *oeuvre*. Nonetheless Bataille writes: "But, Sade would still have only stated that truth [that passion ties us to the divine moment in which being is annihilated] halfway if he had not by his last will and testament given proof of his last fidelity."[8] A return from Apollinaire's version to the actual will leaves us with a mere "halfway statement."

If Sade himself could only pronounce the deadly truth "halfway," his monstrous characters, according to Bataille, attain to the full recklessness of sovereignty. Bataille proposes *Les 120 Journées de Sodome* as Sade's most virulent text, citing descriptions of the libertines in that novel at length (see "Secret II," p. 312) to show how totally unattractive they are. He wishes to demonstrate how Sade reaches a certain *insouciance* by depicting characters lacking in any human virtue, in any humanity at all. Such monstrous characters, in true Bataillian sovereignty, deny "solidarity in relation to all others."[9] Bataille never

mentions that Sade throughout 120 *Journées* refers to
the four libertine masters as "the friends" and that
they display unfailing loyalty and candor in regard
to each other, never betraying the pact implied by
friendship. These four friends could be described as
negating *autrui*, "except nevertheless for the small
number of those who did try to love [them]."

Following Bataille's analysis of 120 *Journées*,
one would expect to find some sort of wild unleashing, with no vestige of respect for the rights of others.
Such is certainly the philosophy the libertines set
forth in their discourse, but a cursory examination of
the structures of the society at Silling Castle reveals
a rigidly ordered life, where it is determined whose
lives will be sacrificed and whose will be saved according to an upside-down but noncapricious system
of rewards for merit.

Before the group arrives at Silling, three of the
four friends exchange their daughters in marriage:
the one exception is the bishop, who cannot marry.
Since the bishop can be an equal member of the
group without marrying simply by offering up his
daughter for prostitution by all the others, the question arises why any of the marriages are necessary at
all. Describing the marriages, Sade writes: "The three
marriages were concluded without delay, the dow-
ries were immense and the clauses equal" (13:2–3).
The marriages, in keeping with their normal function
in the French upper-class society of which the book's
heroes are members, serve to tie men (families) together.[10] As Sade writes, "The association of our four
friends only became all the more stable" (13:4).
Sade's outrageous heroes obey the same imperative
as the historical nobility, marrying to enhance and
consolidate their power. Bataille seeks to separate the

sovereign man depicted in Sade's novels from real, historical sovereigns by saying that while real sovereigns gain power through reciprocal loyalty, Sade's heroes' power "is not limited by any obligation. There is no longer any loyalty which would bind this sovereign to those who give him power" ("Homme souverain," p. 193). On the contrary, the power the friends have at Silling is only possible because of their "stable association."

Instead of the "unbridled freedom" ("Homme souverain," p. 190) by which Bataille characterizes sovereignty, the inhabitants of Silling regulate their life through a complex system of rules, which not only serves to subjugate the victims and thus enhance the libertines' pleasure, but sometimes causes the friends to revolt against the code they drew up and now find too constraining. All murders have been forbidden until the fourth month in the interest of a gradual buildup from simple crimes to the most violent. On the twenty-seventh day of the second month two of the friends get carried away in their passionate anger against one girl. "They propose to give four hundred louis to the society in order to have control of her right that very evening, they were refused [on leur refuse]" (13:364). The impersonality of "on leur refuse" represents the fact that two of the friends are capable of keeping the other two from doing what they wish, because it is not two friends but the society (an impersonal institution) which refuses. In fact, the proposal of four hundred louis is already a sign, even before the refusal, that the libertines, far from free, are confined by their subordination to "the society."

Even a majority of the masters is not sufficient to command an act contrary to the rules. By the twenty-fourth day of the third month the restriction against murder has become exceedingly difficult to bear. "[Curval] conspires with the Duke to take [Augustine] down to the cellar [where the murders are to take place] right that very evening, and they say to Durcet that if they are allowed to do it, they will allow Durcet to expedite Adelaide right away also, but the bishop harangues and gets them to continue to wait for the sake of their pleasure" (13:384). One friend is powerful enough to subdue the three others combined, because that single libertine is in accord with the code of laws. The four friends have alienated their liberty to the rules that they themselves drafted, to "the society." Any talk of freedom by these four monsters is offset by their obvious dependence on loyalty to the pact between them.

In *120 Journées*, the heroes' conduct is unquestionably extreme; the extent of coprolagnia and the incidence of torture and murder for pleasure may well constitute "the most impure account that ever existed" as the narrator (13:60) and Bataille ("Secret II," p. 305) say it does. Nonetheless, the action depicted in this novel lies within the register of civilized, socialized man, where, as Bataille says, "man's respect for man engages him in a cycle of servitude, where there remain only subordinated moments."[11] Bataille has not mistakenly chosen this novel as Sade's most extreme. The subjugation of even the most outrageous libertine to a social contract is a moment found in all of Sade's works, and thus should be considered essential to the portrait of the Sadian monster.

Reminiscent of the scenes of frustrated murder described above is the moment in *La Nouvelle Justine* when Justine has arrived at the convent, and

Jérôme, the oldest and most degenerate of the monks, desires to kill her. Jérôme has no recourse but to plead his case before his brother libertines, whom he asks: "Is it thus for anything else than to satisfy our passions that these bitches live among us?" (6:331). According to Bataille's version of Sade's characters, this would be a rhetorical question, to which the only answer would be the pure affirmation of their monstrous unleashing, the response of the "perfect, inevitably mute, solitude."

In fact, Jérôme, who asks the question in expectation of an affirmative answer, attempts to strengthen his position by referring to the book of laws the monks have written to regulate their mastery: "Let our eyes be open upon the wisest of laws that we have ourselves imposed upon ourselves. I open the book, and I read: 'Should one of the members of the society desire, simply for his satisfaction, the death of all subjects composing the different harems of the house, it will be forbidden any of his colleagues to resist him, and all, by common consent, will flock to favor his desires' " (6:331). This law declares the possibility of an "expenditure without reserve," a "useless loss," the glorious exuberance of sovereignty as outlined in Bataille's general economy.[12] The sovereign man asserts his solitude by denying his dependence upon his victims, by laughing at the prospect of the destruction of *all* the objects of his pleasure. Bataille's sovereign thus is distinguished from Hegel's master, who is locked into a dialectic through the necessity for recognition by his slaves.[13] However, the sovereignty that Jérôme, the law, and Bataille affirm is denied by the very necessity of Jérôme's recourse to the book of laws and of his plea to convince his fellows to agree with him and grant him his desire.

The supposed freedom is ironically undermined by its implication in a parody of democratic process. The parody follows democratic procedure to the letter, and in its very literal fidelity exposes not the lack of democracy in this libertine society, but the lack of true, unbridled liberty in any democracy: democracy being the realm where liberty is legislated.

Jérôme's motion is immediately seconded by Clément. Then Severino, the convent's superior, takes the floor. "I know our laws as well as Jérôme—says Severino, phlegmatically—but, while citing the article that favors his desires, he forgot the one which can constrain them. I open the book to the same article, and I find following what he read to you: 'It will nevertheless be enforced that we proceed to the judgment of the discredited subject only after a majority vote'" (6:331). A vote follows Severino's speech and Jérôme's motion is defeated by a count of four to two. Once again it is not mere majority, mere superiority of force that carries the decision, but recourse to a code of laws where majority is declared the deciding factor. Although the law Jérôme reads appears to affirm each libertine's sovereignty, the fact that sovereignty must be affirmed by codified law means that the freedom of each libertine is subordinated to his loyalty to a pact.

The third code of laws for immoral conduct in the work of Sade appears in the episode of *Juliette* in which the heroine is inducted by her friend Clairwil into "The Society of Friends of Crime." The thirteenth statute of this society decrees that no cruel passion, except the thong applied to the buttocks, should be practiced between the brothers of the society. In community seraglios the friends of crime will be supplied with victims for their cruel and murderous passions (8:403–404). The thirty-second statute of that code of laws forbids murder between the brothers of the order, although it allows theft (8:406). Most surprisingly, the eighth statute reads: "The friends in this society, united as if in the bosom of a family, share all their pains as well as all their pleasures; they mutually aid and succor each other in all life's different situations" (8:403).

Although the "Society" forms the backdrop for only a small portion of Juliette's adventures, its code of laws governs her conduct throughout her many exploits. Traveling through Italy, she and her companions (Sbrigani and two subalterns, one male and one female) are led by the cruel, solitary giant Minski to his castle. During their stay at Minski's, the seven-foot–three-inch libertine begs and obtains Juliette's permission to sacrifice both of her domestics to his passion. Juliette and Sbrigani realize their own peril and decide they must escape. Although she has poison in her possession and has not hesitated to kill on numerous prior occasions, Juliette refuses to kill the man who threatens her life. Such a decision must be based upon some ethical code. Juliette tells Sbrigani, in words echoing the statutes of the Society of Friends of Crime, "It will not be the friend of crime who destroys crime's partisan. He must be robbed, that is essential" (9:18).

The Society serves as a paradigm for the entire *Histoire de Juliette*. Although the libertines have not formally entered into a pact of mutual assistance, the pact is understood. Throughout the book whenever one libertine destroys another, the excuse is always given that the murdered character was not sufficiently

outrageous in her passions.[14] The monstrous libertines in the words of Sade are always found in
groups. Even the cruelest character becomes more
sympathetic as we see him in the role of friend.
Friends are betrayed,[15] but excuses are always given.
Brother criminals are never destroyed capriciously,
as are victims, although undifferentiated capricious
destruction is what one would expect from Bataille's
description of "Sade's system." Bataille writes: "The
negation of partners is, according to [Sade], the fun-
damental piece in the system" ("Homme souverain,"
p. 185).

The one exception to the fraternity of libertines
is Minski. Although he provides hospitality to Juliette, he would sacrifice her to a whim. Minski is the
limit point of Sade's work, the least human, most
sovereign of his characters. Not only does he stand
seven feet three inches tall, but Minski is endowed
with a penis measuring eighteen inches in length
and sixteen in circumference, which is always erect,
"even while sleeping, even while walking" (8:560).
Far surpassing all of Sade's other characters in his
threat to verisimilitude, Miniski is the accomplishment of the impossible.

The Russian giant operates alone, unlike Sade's
other libertines. Minski is the exception that proves
how far Sade's other monsters are from the sovereignty Bataille ascribes to them. Yet even in Minski's
self-portrait there erupts a note of melancholy and
loneliness when, having been asked if he had been
his family's executioner, he replies: "Alas, I missed
my father, that's what grieves me: I was too young
when he died. But all the rest have passed away by
my hands. I already told you of the death of my
mother and sister; I would have liked to see them

reborn to have the pleasure of massacring them again; I am rather unhappy now since there are only ordinary victims left to sacrifice: my heart is blunted, I no longer get any pleasure" (8:575–76). Even Minski does not fulfill the description of the sovereign man that Bataille quotes from Blanchot: "If he lives, there is no event of his existence that he cannot experience as fortunate."[16]

Unlike Minski, the rest of Sade's libertines openly enjoy the pleasures of friendship. In *Juliette*, Clairwil declares "Let it be known, when you are no longer here, that the charms of tender friendship find partisans, even in the bosom of debauchery" (9:217; see also 9:312). Even happy marriages are found when both partners are equally corrupt. For example, the d'Estervals, whom Justine encounters in *La Nouvelle Justine*, have a marriage described by the narrator as follows: "The most perfect union reigned nonetheless in this couple, as corrupt as they could be: how false it is to say that it is only the virtuous associations which endure" (7:100).

The "stable association" among the four friends of *120 Journées*, which is exemplary of a looser, but no less certain, fraternity between libertines throughout Sade's books, is only one aspect of the comfortable, humane side of that outrageous novel. The other manifestation of human solidarity is the fact that twelve people besides the four friends return from Silling Castle and that in all twelve cases, survival is a well-merited reward promised and delivered. It is set down in the *Règlements* for the four months that "talents must always be respected" (13:55). The twelve survivors consist of the four "fuckers" with the biggest virile members (rewarded for their talent), the three cooks ("because of their talents"—13:429), the four storytellers[17] and Julie, the Duke's daughter and Curval's wife. Julie is the only character to survive in spite of her classification. On the twenty-first day of the first month Julie actually joins the ranks of the storytellers: "The Duke and Curval . . . spent the night drinking with the four storytellers and Julie, whose libertinage, increasing every day, caused her to be considered a very likeable creature and one who deserved reckoning among the objects who were shown consideration" (13:270–71). Here is evidence of a standard of immorality by which a person can be judged meritorious and rewarded with consideration. The consideration means that Julie has joined the fraternity of libertines and can depend upon the friends' fidelity to their words. In the same way, at the end of the month, the storyteller for the month is paid for her services (and her properly corrupt attitude) by being promised survival. The promise is honored.[18]

Although he has defined Sade's sovereign man as free from obligation to others, Bataille does find that the sovereign is nonetheless constrained by the obligation to be sovereign, that is, to measure up to some idea of sovereignty. "Free in front of other people he is nonetheless the victim of his own sovereignty. He is not free to accept a servitude such as seeking a paltry sensual pleasure, he is not free to stoop! What is remarkable is that Sade, beginning with a perfect disloyalty, nonetheless ends up with rigor" ("Homme souverain," p. 193). This "perfect disloyalty" is used to describe those brothers of the fraternity of libertines who "mutually aid and succor each other." The "rigor" Bataille finds is actually maintained in Sade's novels either by admonitions from more accomplished libertines to apprentices, or by obedience to a code of laws which has been written precisely to keep libertines from subordinating their criminality to their desires.

For Bataille this "rigor" stems from the Sadian libertine's victimization to his own sovereignty. Following a logic of pure destruction which subjugates any personal desire for destruction, Bataille ends up with a sovereign man who is sworn to his own destruction. Thus the sovereignty of Sade's characters marks them for a course leading to the "definitive silence" (a solitary rigor, unmediated self-destruction, an heroic code) which Bataille maintains as the crowning achievement of Sade's text, as represented in the faulty version of the last will and testament which Bataille read.

This pure negativity is unlivable, impossible. Bataille declares that impossibility throughout his different studies on Sade,[19] for its unmitigated impossibility makes this a true sovereignty, not the hollow sovereignty of the historical ruler. Yet Bataille leaves a loophole by which Sade can obtain that which no person can wish for, and which Sade himself can only demand covertly.[20] Bataille's loophole is fiction and its capacity for realizing the impossible. Sade "put to use the unlimited nature of literature. . . . Sade imagined the exorbitant privileges . . . that would have been usurped by the villainy of the great lords and kings, endowed by novelistic fiction, with omnipotence and impunity" ("Homme souverain," p. 185).

Bataille's case for Sade rests upon the execution of a clean cut between the author's life and the author's work. Sade the man loved like any other, acted politically in the interests of the people, and cried "tears of blood" over the loss of a manuscript (see

"Homme souverain," pp. 187–88). Sade lived a possible life: "Sade, himself, no doubt had neither the strength nor the audacity to reach the supreme moment he has described" ("Homme souverain," p. 190). But Bataille's Sade is unsurpassed in force and audacity when describing that supreme moment. For Bataille, Sade lived a possible life, but wrote an impossible life.

Bataille never questions Sade's success in depicting sovereignty, but he does examine the contradiction of Sade's crying over the loss of a manuscript "where he attempted to reveal—to *other men*—the truth of the insignificance of others" ("Homme souverain," p. 188). Bataille locates the contradiction between the form and content of Sade's text; it is a contradiction between the very fact of writing, i.e., wanting-to-be-read, and writing a negation of *autrui*. This external contradiction can be replaced by one internal to the work—the contradiction between the libertines' declarations of their complete freedom based upon a heedlessness in regard to other people and their continuing submission to the contract underlying the society of libertines.

In reference to the libertine characters' dissertations on their sovereignty, Bataille asserts that "these dissertations . . . are not the dissertations of the violent characters to whom they have been lent. If such characters had lived, no doubt they would have lived silently. These are the words of Sade himself, who used this method to address himself *to others*" ("Homme normal," p. 208). These cannot be the speeches of the sovereign men that Bataille declares Sade's characters to be. The simple fact of discourse with others is antithetical to sovereignty.[21] To conserve the sovereignty of Sade's characters, Bataille

must assign their discourse to "Sade himself," that is
to Sade the person who is a humanist, rather than to
Sade the writer who "never . . . represented anything
except as unlivable, *impossible*" ("Secret II," p. 312).
What is left of these heroes, once denuded of their
language, are their acts, which, as we have seen, are
inscribed within an ethical code that subordinates
the individual libertine's freedom to his loyalty to
the principles of the fraternity of "friends of crime."
The sovereign man that Bataille finds in Sade's novels neither acts nor speaks in a sovereign manner.

Bataille displaces the locus of sovereignty from
Sade to Sade's heroes, and then to those heroes as
they *ought* to be, as opposed to how they are por-
trayed in Sade's books. One Sadian character, Amélie,
who in her wish to be destroyed by Borchamps—to be
the cause of a crime in her death—supports Bataille's
construct of sovereignty entailing a will to self-anni-
hilation.[22] Yet in the *Histoire de Juliette*, Amélie never
lives up to her declared wish. She proves jealous,
timid, and fearful for her life (See 9:276–80). Sovereignty is not to be found in Sade nor in Sade's heroes. Nonetheless, Sade somehow provides Bataille
with the possibility for a dissertation on sovereignty,
on the impossible. Sovereignty does not belong to the
life that bears the name Sade, nor to the texts ascribed to that name, but, as Bataille writes, "the *figure*
Sade, assuredly, is incompatible with any concur-
rence by those moved by need and fear" ("Homme
normal," p. 194).

Bataille gives us his explanation of just such a
process as this attribution of sovereignty to the
"figure Sade" when neither Sade nor his creations
are sovereign: "It often—the most often—seems to
me that real personages only give their flesh, and the

virulence of their character, to possibilities surpassing what they truly are. And so we should never
speak of them separately, but at the same time as the
dream beings begot by mythology or fiction. Sade is
not only the exceptional man: . . . Sade is also a
thought if not of the people then of the crowd."[23] By
uniting Sade with mythological or fictional beings,
Bataille endows Sade with "the omnipotence and
impunity" proper to "novelistic fiction." "A thought
of the crowd" is precisely how Bataille describes the
function of the sovereign in ancient times when "the
ancient game would have it that the *spectacle* of
royal privileges compensated the poverty of common
life" (see "Homme souverain," pp. 182-84). Bataille
crowns the "figure Sade" sovereign so that it may
realize that which is impossible for any living person, for any possible writer.

Sovereignty has undergone another relocation,
this time from the Sadian fictional character to a
fictional Sade, begotten by the dream of the crowd,
for whom Bataille is the spokeman. In his function
as advocate of that dream Bataille must suppress a
facet of Sade that is represented by the prevalence of
friendship among his monstrous heroes, operating a
number of similar excisions in order to present a
sovereign figure of Sade.

Just as he publicizes the solitude and ignores the
society in Sade's novels, Bataille's tactics also include denial of the attraction of Sade's texts in favor
of their repulsiveness. In his deposition at the trial of
Editions Jean-Jacques Pauvert for the crime of having
published Sade's most outrageous works, Bataille de-
fends those books from being labeled pornography
by saying that "most of the time, anyone trying his
hand at reading Sade would rather find himself sick-

ened with horror."[24] Although such a statement might be attributed to Bataille's interest in supporting the publication of Sade's works, ten years earlier Bataille had written that "the celebrations at Silling would repulse the most disciplined fakirs: and if someone claimed to desire the life of these unfortunates, full of blood and nauseating, they would be boasting wretchedly indeed. ... there is no ascetic who has overcome disgust to that degree" ("Secret II," p. 305).

Much of the behavior in Sade's novels is disgusting, and very few readers would feel tempted to use them as models for their life. But the sexual arousal produced by reading Sade cannot be ignored. Bataille plays down the attractive, titillating side of Sade, because he feels the violence of Sade lies in the ability to elicit repulsion. Yet the virulence of a reading of Sade stems from the mixture of disgust and arousal the reader feels. Pornographic status cannot be denied by affirming a capacity to horrify. On the contrary, in Sade the disgusting and the terrifying are sexy. The libertine Belmor exposes the complicity between disgust and desire in an address to the Society of Friends of Crime upon the occasion of his installation as president of the society: "Is not resistance thus the very soul of desire: in that case where can it exist more completely than at the heart of disgust?"[25]

In a move analogous to the sanction of disgust at the expense of attraction, Bataille posits an ideal reader of Sade: the "normal man" who misunderstands and misjudges Sade. Bataille thinks that the normal man's disgust and horror in response to Sade are closer to a true response than the admiration which is beginning to be expressed for the marquis.

The reader who condemns Sade as a villain is a necessary complement to a work whose meaning, according to Bataille, is revulsion ("Homme normal," p. 199). The admirer of Sade, by accepting Sade into the human community, denies Sade the function of spokesman for the "silent life" and the "perfect solitude." Bataille holds that the words of Sade cannot be received, that to hear them is essentially to misunderstand them: "Only the misunderstanding of the mass of men, and their disgust can be the effect deserved by Sade's ideas. But at least this misunderstanding keeps the essential, whereas the admiration of a small number, which is nowadays granted him, is less the consequence than the desire, for it does not demand the solitude of the voluptuary" ("Homme normal," p. 221).

Are not the "small number" of admirers of Sade today the descendants of the "small number of those who did try to love me" to whom Sade refers in that portion of his last will and testament which Bataille has not read? Do not these two avatars of the "small number" respond to a less violent side of Sade's work? They correspond to the "small number" who survive the orgies of *120 Journées* because of their talents. They are the result of the small minority of people in the world of Sade's novels who pass the initiation rites of the fraternity of friends of crime. In order to maintain Sadian sovereignty, Bataille is forced to banish the exception, the "small number," wherever he finds it furtively eroding the "perfect solitude" of the "figure Sade."

Through the different manifestations of his dismissal of the human, livable aspect of Sade, Bataille exercises a passage to the limit upon the Sadian figure and the Sadian text, transforming the work of negativity and violence in Sade into pure negativity, definitive silence. Bataille contrasts the purity of Sadian sexuality with the watered-down version found in human existence: "We must be grateful to Sade, for making *volupté* the only truth and the only measure, for never confusing it with *agrément*" ("Vue d'ensemble," p. 992). *Le Petit Robert*[26] defines *volupté* as "1. *Keen* pleasure of the senses, enjoyment *fully tasted*. 2. Sexual pleasure. 3. *Very keen* intellectual or esthetic pleasure" (p. 1924, my italics). "Sexual pleasure," unadorned by any quantitative modifiers, can be equated to other forms of pleasure (*volupté*'s other definitions) only if those pleasures are specified as "very keen" or "fully tasted." The attribution of sexuality is sufficient to imply extremes of intensity. In this emphasis on the excessive, on the violent intensity, is located the "only truth" and the "only measure" for Sade and the sovereign man.

Volupté is characterized by the exceeding of a certain quantitative level. The prevalence of quantification and categorization and the vast number of victims in Sade's text account for Sade's unprecedented success in doing violence to humanistic notions of man's dignity and individuality. The Sadian hero appears as someone with an insatiable quota to fill, someone with a heroic task which does not afford him any simple pleasure.

Agrément has three definitions, all of which Bataille excludes from his reading of Sade: "1. Permission, approval emanating from an authority. 2. Quality of a thing, of a being which makes them pleasant. 3. Pleasure (in certain expressions): '*Propriété d'agrément*' [property for pleasure] (as opposed to: *de rapport* [for profit]); '*Jardin d'agrément*' [garden for pleasure] (as opposed to: kitchen garden); 'Voyage d'agrément' (as opposed to: business trip)" (*Petit Robert*, p. 34). Bataille finds in Sade a violent sexual pleasure that does not bow to any authority (cares not for the first meaning of *agrément*) and does not subordinate itself to the necessity of being pleasant and agreeable (is indifferent to the second sense). Not only does this exclusion of the *agrément* leave no place for the criminal societies with their codes of law or for the happy moments of agreeable company, delicious food, and lovely victims, but it neglects the perversity implicit in *agrément*. When *agrément* means pleasure (third definition), *d'agrément* always indicates something in opposition to utility.

The definition of *agrément* slides from a proper subservience to authority into a general insubordination to any rule, even that of one's own interests. The central definition (agreeableness that is inherent in an object), which appears to have no relation to permission or approval, is actually a turning point in the relation to some transcendant hierarchic principle which would subordinate to its own ends any charm that is merely immanent in a thing. The moment of innocent pleasantness marks the start of a perverse insubordination to any external approval or authority. The possibility for simple, self-contained pleasure which makes no reference to permission or morality is the germ of the explicit opposition to utility of the third definition. The pleasure of *agrément* lies in a silent, stealthy subversion of the utilitarian goal of a restricted economy: the economy Bataille would exceed with his "general economy." *Volupté*, with its emphasis upon intensity, maintains the unity and selfsameness of "sexual pleasure," which unlike other pleasures needs no qualifications, is always identical in its pure intensity. In contrast to that, Sade's writing, with all its variations and refinements, gradations and delicacies, poses the multiplicity of sexual pleasures, in which sexual pleasure knows different degrees of intensity.

Agrément and *volupté* intersect in the notion of pleasure. To ensure that *volupté* is not contaminated by amenity, the intense pleasure must be so violently extreme it is no longer pleasure but simply pure intensity. Actual sexual intercourse is a compromise, an impure half-measure between communion and destruction, between amenities and violent intensity (see "Bonheur," p. 404). Bataille says that life, the register of the possible, necessitates compromised sexuality, whereas Sade's fiction makes possible the revelation of "the true nature of sexual attraction," that is, violence, which in life remains hidden behind "the fog of affection" ("Bonheur," p. 405).

When the fog has lifed, the pure sexual (sexual intensity devoid of pleasure) reveals itself as pure destruction. This uncompromised negation might be an attribute of sovereignty, but it is not characteristic of the sexuality in Sade's fiction. The violence presented in Sade's text is not separated from fondness, from love, but subverts the purity of affection by revealing the later's complicity with aggressivity: "Rodin, drunk with love and ferocity, mixes once again the expressions and sentiments of both" (*Nouvelle Justine*, 6:237). The friends in *120 Journées* fall in love with certain members of their harem who become their favorites. The death of a pet is more intensely desired than any other. Minski's melancholy in regard to the loss of his entire family manifests this solitary giant's need for a special victim, set apart by ties of affection, in order to guarantee the enormity of his crime.

The outrageous quality of sexuality in Sade stems not from unleashing violence from the bonds of affection, but from mixing love with the greatest ferocity. Undifferentiated violence, pure negativity, would not pierce through the "fog of affection" as successfully as does violence directed at the loved one. Thus incest in Sade is not the loosing of a polymorphous perversity that is heedless to society's categories, but the unveiling of a violent passion that is inextricably linked to feelings of familial tenderness. "Let a father, let a brother, idolizing his daughter or sister, descend to the depths of his soul, and interrogate himself scrupulously about what he feels: he will see if that pious affection is anything other than the desire to fuck" (*Nouvelle Justine*, 7:183). Not only are members of the libertine fraternity "united as if in the bosom of a family" (*Juliette*, 8:403), but the interaction in the bosom of the family is as potentially outrageous as within the Society of Friends of Crime.

It is the chimeralike composite of *agrément* and *volupté* that constitutes Sade's assault upon normal man. In this mutual contamination the innocence of amenity becomes possessed with a violent intensity, exposing the perverse potentials of such a lack of tendentiousness.[27] And the intensity which is the seriousness of *volupté* becomes intolerable by being deflected onto everything, onto the innocent little pleasures of everyday life. The result is not pure violence, but the violently impure, monstrously (monstrous in the way that a chimera is a terrifying composite of parts proper to different creatures) unwieldy Sadian text.

2 | Friends / Corpses / Turds / Whores: Blanchot on Sade

> I guessed the extreme desire he had to make me eat his shit; I anticipated it: I asked him permission to do it, he was wild with joy.
> —Juliette in *Juliette* (8:227)

THE operation by which Georges Bataille writes the name Sade, by which he invokes the figure Sade to come and accompany his text, entails long quotations from and frequent references to Bataille's friend Maurice Blanchot. At the same time Bataille's reading consistently ignores an entire aspect of Sade which relates to friendship. Rather than friendship—that highly moral, systematically principled word—I should, following Roland Barthes's example, simply say friends: "*l'amitié* [friendship], or rather (since that Latin version word is too rigid, too prudish): *des amis* [friends] (speaking of them, I can never but grasp myself, grasp them in a contingency—a difference)."[1] The lighter, friendlier, more livable side of Sade appears in the form of a small number of exceptions to the rigidity of his categorical imperatives.

Bataille thus reenacts the typical Sa-

dian scene: brother libertines come together and, in
the comfort of good company, discourse upon the
nothingness of *autrui*, upon the absolute solitude
that is the basis of man's liberty and energy. Although his reading of Sade bears the imprint of a
certain community of readers—Maurice Heine, Jean
Paulhan, Pierre Klossowski, and, most of all, Blanchot—Bataille nonetheless denounces the small cir-
cle of Sade's modern-day admirers as a perversion of
Sade's effect and force.

Unlike Bataille, Blanchot, in his articles on Sade,
explicitly discusses the various communities of libertines. His first mention of Sadian friends empha-
sizes the puzzle inherent in any relations between
such absolute egoists: "The relations between these
peerless men are rather equivocal."[2] The libertines
make alliances, marry each other's daughters, and
recognize each other's power, but do not actually
care about each other, not even about each other's
demise. In "Quelques remarques sur Sade," Blanchot's first piece on Sade, this impasse is reached and
then bypassed through a detour into *Les Liaisons
dangereuses*. Sade's libertines are not like Merteuil
and Valmont, not engaged together in a death struggle for ascendancy. By the end of the digression, the
equivocation is no longer in sight: "The fact is that
this society of heroes only illustrates the complete
solitude of each one of them" (p. 245). The relations
are no longer puzzling; the general rule that the Sadian hero does not recognize the existence of *autrui*
has been reinstated.

The dilemma of Sadian alliances has not been
settled, merely avoided, and thus it returns in full
force in the next Blanchot piece on Sade, "La Raison
de Sade."[3] In that article, structured like an Hegelian

dialectic, each moment of conflict is resolved and sublated into another moment. Having just reduced to naught any obstacle to the purely negative relation between powerful libertine and insignificant victim, Blanchot then says that the true problem is that of the relations between each absolute power (p. 25). These unique, solitary figures join together in groups because "their similar tastes bring them together." Blanchot is not describing merely cold and formal social alliances, but true complicities of affinity. "But what could be the relation of the exception to the exception? Certainly this question much preoccupied Sade." "La Raison de Sade" reaches the momentary conclusion that "superior libertines ally themselves, but do not encounter each other" (p. 26).

However, Blanchot with his dialectical method need not ignore these friendships; he simply arranges the mess of unembarrassed contradictions in Sade's work into a neat dialectical progress: "As always, [Sade] goes from one solution to another, so that finally, at the end of his logic, he discloses the only answer to this riddle that matters to him." Having convincingly set up the possibility that the great libertines refrain from injuring each other so as not to endanger their power, Blanchot asks whether here, then, remains one principle, one prohibition, for these reckless strivers after criminal perfection. Finally Blanchot reaches "the answer to the riddle": "Truly his work is strewn with the corpses of libertines, struck down at the summit of their glory" (p. 27). Libertines kill other libertines; there is no last inviolable principle. The obscure puzzle has revealed its truth. In Hegelian terms, the standpoint of the naive consciousness has given way to the perspective of absolute knowledge—"truly." Now the

knot of equivocal relations between peers can be
confidently left behind.

The article by Blanchot, which Bataille dismem-
bers, was entitled "A la rencontre de Sade [to encounter Sade]," a title that was changed (when the
essay was published in *Lautréamont et Sade*) to "La
Raison de Sade [Sade's Reason]." Since the rhythm
and structure of "La Raison de Sade" is patterned
after the *Phenomenology of Mind*, the movement towards ("à la rencontre de") Sade progresses towards
an absolute knowledge that would not be the dead
abstraction of literary history. Throughout the *Phenomenology* the corpse continually appears as the
mark of some abstract, nondialectical negation. This
is the negation that affirms nothing, the impasse of
any moment of the dialectical progress viewed from
a position outside of absolute knowledge, from the
position of the naive consciousness. The dynamic
force of incessant negation freezes, in any moment
taken out of context, into empty negativity. The
corpse is the outcome of the death struggle for recognition before that is sublated into the master / slave
dialectic. In discussing the dead end of absolute freedom Hegel writes: "The sole and only work and deed
accomplished by universal freedom is therefore
death—a death that achieves nothing, embraces
nothing within its grasp. . . . It is thus the most
coldblooded and meaningless death of all, with no
more significance than cleaving a head of cabbage or
swallowing a draught of water."[4] Bataille's operation
of taking sections out of Blanchot causes him to present dead moments of Blanchot's dialectical process:
corpses which, when cut off from the restless negation that gives them life, are other than themselves
in their very stillness. Thus just as Sade's work is

"strewn with the corpses of libertines, struck down at the summit of their glory," this dismemberment of Blanchot, in an attempt at appropriation, is the movement of striking down a friend, a brother libertine, "at the summit of [his] glory."[5]

After Bataille's actual death, Blanchot explicitly confronts the violence of such an appropriation in an article (about the impossibility of an article) about Georges Bataille, entitled "L'Amitié." "Friendship . . . submits to the recognition of the common strangeness which does not allow us to speak of our friends, but only to speak to them, not to make of them the theme of conversations (or articles). . . . In this, discretion is not in the simple refusal to disclose confidences . . . but is . . . the pure interval . . . the interruption of being which never authorizes me to dispose of him, nor of my knowledge of him (even were it to praise him)."[6]

A major and a minor mode of friendship are to be distinguished. For Barthes, friendship's radical mode means that "speaking of [friends], I can never but grasp myself, grasp them in a contingency—a difference." Blanchot, likewise, locates contingency, the unforeseeable, as the interval, the separation, in which is situated the link between friends. This interval ("interruption of being"), this difference or contingency, can also be expressed as the unforeseeable possibility of death: not death that happens at some unforeseen moment, but death as absolutely unforeseeable, absolutely exterior to any image. This radical exteriority makes its presence felt in speech. "What is present in this presence of speech . . . is precisely what never lets itself be seen nor reached: something is here, which is out of reach . . . ; it is between us, it stands between [*se tient entre*], and

conversation [l'entretien] is the approach which begins with this intermediate space [entre-deux], an
irreducible distance that must be preserved if we
wish to maintain the relation to the unknown which
is the unique gift of speech."[7]

The distinction between "speak of our friends"
and "speak to them" is tied to the question of respect
for the pure interval, the irreducible distance. Likewise, Nietzsche sets up a strong notion of the friend
through the opposition near and far. Zarathustra ad-
vises not love of thy neighbor, or the near (Nächsten-
liebe), but of the far (Fersten-liebe). The friend is the
relation to the far: "Do I advise you to neighbor-love
[Nächsten-liebe]? Rather do I advise you to neighbor-
flight and to furthest love [Fernsten-liebe]? . . . Not
the neighbor do I teach you, but the friend."[8] That
which is most interior to intimacy, that which is
between, is the ultimate exteriority ("out of reach").
Blanchot would respect that exteriority which is the
very heart, the innermost, of any intimacy. The minor
mode of friendship is the register of proximity and
possession. The plural difference of friends honors
the "words from one shore to the other shore"
(L'Amitié, p. 329), does not try to cross the irreducible distance with the "ship" of friendship.

Propre death (propre: own, same, selfsame,
proper, appropriate, good, right, correct, clean, neat,
tidy),[9] the corpse that is there, the remains of Blanchot's writing neatly inserted into the ground of Bataille's work, does not respect the interval, the
intimate exteriority, constitutive of the relation between friends. "Thus death has the false virtue of
appearing to bring back to intimacy those who were
divided by grave differences. With it there is a disappearance of everything that separates" (L'Amitié,

p. 329). *Propre* death, death in its minor mode, is the destruction of the unbridgeable distance necessarily separating friends—that distance which is the unforeseeable possibility, the potential for the unforeseeable, "what never lets itself be seen nor reached": death in its major mode.[10] Yet the corpse is both the possibility of image (the tangibility of the absolutely foreseeable, the constitution of the identical) and a link to the impossibility of image (an image of death as absolute exteriority, "a relation to the unknown"). "Death suspends the relationship to place. . . . The corpse is not in its place. Where is it? It is not here and yet it is not elsewhere; nowhere? but then nowhere is here. The corpse's presence establishes a link between here and nowhere."[11]

Sade's work, "strewn with corpses," is strewn with that which is and is not in its place, which is always a reference to that which disturbs the stasis of place, strewn with traces of that which is not there or anywhere. Bataille's reading of Sade is likewise riddled with holes that mark a relation to the unknown, to the radical exteriority that is the "intermediate space" between friends. The excerpted sections of Blanchot, instead of being that which is most appropriable, most easily circumscribed, are monuments to the impossibility of circumscription: impossible because exteriority is that which is innermost. The equivocal nature of friendship in Sade, which Blanchot explicitly confronts and Bataille does not, plays itself out in Bataille's text as the fiction of a peaceful coexistence of two texts, whose relation is never articulated. In Sade "superior libertines ally themselves, but do not encounter each other" (*L&S*, p. 26). Thus, Bataille and Blanchot (at any rate the writings bearing those names) are Sadian heroes.

The corpses littering Sade's work (and the pieces of Blanchot lying about in Bataille's text) are at once absolutely still, able to be disposed of, identical to themselves (that is to say, *propre*), and essentially improper, by being a link to that which is absolutely inappropriable, that which tauntingly exceeds the libertine's grasp. The corpse, the supreme monument to the libertine's victory and mastery, is itself also the sign of the limits of his domain, of his ultimate impotence. Blanchot would read the corpses as only minor mode, would dismiss them as too tame. He writes with unusually disrespectful imperiousness: "We are leaving aside the stories of necrophilia which, although numerous enough in Sade, seem rather far away from the 'normal' possibilities of his heroes" (*L&S*, p. 34). The gesture of "leaving aside" is the move of disposal—disposing of the corpse, putting it in its place. The putting into quotation marks of "normal" does not deny the domesticating, centralizing tendency of Blanchot's reading. It merely serves to mark the categories "normal" and "abnormal" with the knowing wink of Hegel as he distinguishes between the for-itself (for the naive consciousness) and the in-itself (for us—the philosophers). The categories are no less seriously in play, but their *Aufhebung* is assumed.[12]

Blanchot goes on to say that what the libertines who get aroused by corpses are actually enjoying is simply a verification of their potency as murderers: the titillating corpses are their own ex-victims. For Blanchot, it is the infinite energy of negation that is everything in Sade. "This negation . . . which no particular instance can satisfy, is essentially destined to go beyond the plane of human existence" (*L&S*, p. 34). The object, the victim of any particular negation, is already nothing; it has been "preliminarily annihilated" (p. 33). The Sadian libertine destroys any particular person in the context of a preliminary denial of the reality of *autrui*. This preliminary annihilation, necessary preface to any particular negation frees the libertine from being locked into a dialectic of recognition with his victim. This prefatory destruction is Sade in the major mode, irrecoverable, inappropriable death—no one's death, death that is not *propre*. Thus the libertine in his frequent necrophilic violations is, in fact, reenacting in parodic form what Blanchot has delineated as *the* Sadian dialectic: "all the particular cruelties are now merely destined to verify and confirm this universal annihilation" ("Remarques," p. 246). Necrophilic acts are the literal, parodic interpretations of an act of violence upon a victim that has *already* been destroyed, is already nothing. The preliminary, total destruction, which Blanchot means figuratively or metaphysically, is here literally the killing of the victim. To fuck the corpse of a person one has just killed is to attempt to verify and confirm the prefatory annihilation.

Blanchot thus dismisses ("leaving aside") as uninteresting the acts offering the clearest image of the movement he finds central to Sade. These acts *would be* uninteresting if they were mere images, successfully framing and taming something radically exterior. But the corpse is and is not the image of the dead one. It is an opening onto the impossibility of retention or spoils of victory. If Sade, according to Blanchot, has established "as horizon to his destructive project something which goes infinitely beyond them and their little bit of existence" (*L&S*, p. 34), the marker pointing to that beyond is the corpse: "a link between here and nowhere."

The corpse is that which is left over, which exceeds the life and death struggle for recognition in the Hegelian dialectic. It is the monument to the success *and* the impossibility of success of that death struggle. "Through death, doubtless, there has arisen the certainty that both did stake their life, and held it lightly both in their own case and in the case of the other; but that is not for those who underwent this struggle" (*Phen.*, p. 233). It is not for those who underwent this struggle because they are dead. In order for a consciousness to gain something from a negation, the consciousness must survive that negation. Alexandre Kojève comments on this impasse: "It thus is worth nothing to the man of struggle to kill his adversary. He must suppress him 'dialectically.' "[13] The corpse, proof of victory, cannot bear witness to that victory. Hegel goes on to say that the two combatants "cancel themselves and are sublated as terms or extremes seeking to have existence on their own account" (p. 233). When this impasse situation is dialectically suppressed (*aufgehoben*) into the master / slave dialectic, what is left behind is the corpse: the face of the impossibility of recognition, the trace of the irreducible distance.

Blanchot leaves behind the corpses as waste products of the "energetic process" of infinite negation, the movement common to both Sade and Hegel. Of course Blanchot is careful to point out that "Sade isn't Hegel, far from it" (*L'Entretien*, p. 327). Yet the dialectical movement by which Blanchot dismisses the corpse as minor mode, as secondarily negated, is the move to assimilate Sade to Hegel: a direction that is not alien to Sade. The difference between the two is one of irony. Sade too would deny the importance of the corpse by equating it to excrement. However, even more than the corpse, it is excrement in Sade which comes to usurp too central a place.

Olympe de Borghese tells her dear friends (who will later toss her into a volcano) in *L'Histoire de Juliette:* "Let us be well convinced by the system that absolutely nothing of us exists when we are dead, and that these remains, which we leave on this earth, are no more than what our excrement was . . . when we existed" (9:362). We leave behind something to which we give the name "remains," but it is a strange something which is "absolutely nothing." In fact, excrement in Sade is far from being something to be left behind, disposed of, to be put in its place. In the Sadian context, the equation excrement = corpse prolongs the equivocal nature of corpse as at once disposable, circumscribable, forgettable, and as a "relation to the unknown," "a link between here and nowhere": the corpse's presence as a sign of the radical exteriority that is here with us.

In *120 Journées de Sodome*, which presents itself as an encyclopedic account of "all passions" (13:27), coprolagnic passions are so grossly over-represented that the reader is forced to interrogate the supposed project of encyclopedic coverage itself. An effort at scientific impartiality elicits from Gilbert Lély the naively insightful remark that "we must nevertheless take note of the fact that in many places a dominant error comes to compromise the didactic value of such a work: we refer to the monstrously exaggerated place which the author reserves for the coprolagnic aberration carried to its ultimate excesses."[14] In the Sadian universe the very notion of "didactic value" is set askew by the prevalence of teaching as seduction and violation, as temptation to "error." For Lély, the book's value is compromised (like a young lady's honor) by a "monstrous" exaggeration. Coprolagnia in the context of an encyclopedia of perversions is not monstrous, is normal, when it is in its place, properly disposed of. Yet coprolagnia reassumes its status as monstrous by refusing to be disposed of, refusing to keep to its place.

Erotic play with excrement is perverse through the refusal to dispose of it, to put the improper in its place, to leave it behind. In order to maintain its perversity in a context where any perversion is "normal," in a context that *is* the proper place for the improper, coprolagnia manifests itself as that which does not know its place, that which will not be left behind. It comes to pester the other perversions, to invade their place; so we have whipping with shit-eating, buggery with shit-eating, killing with shit-eating. Lély goes on to say: "Besides the monotony which results from this sort of abuse, some of the most compelling cases . . . are in some way fallen [*déchus*], from their universal attribution, because of the coprophagic element that Sade deemed necessary to graft onto the principal perversions" (p. 334). The principal perversions (Blanchot's " 'normal' possibilities of his heroes") are *déchus*, that is to say they have become *déchets*—waste products, turds.

The turd, like the corpse, ought to be left behind in any universal process. *Les 120 Journées* would present itself as a gradual progress from simple passions to some sort of ultimate crime, yet the insistence of coprophagia, cutting across every category, its inability to be surpassed, to be dialectically suppressed, plays itself out as the decay of the book's encyclopedic universality. Lély comments that, although lesser degrees of coprolagnia (pleasure in smelling, pleasure in the apprehension of traces of excrement) are not uncommon, "the coprolagnic aberration carried to its ultimate excesses" (that is, coprophagia) is extremely rare. Just as Blanchot sees the libertines' "normal" focus to be on the traces of the murderous passion, on the potential for murder and not on the corpse as corpse; so too the hint of shit, the trace of shit, ought to be more titillating than the full brute presence of the lifeless turd. The turd is the dead moment fallen out of the digestive process. To eat it is to incorporate that which has already been detached (Bataille's pieces from Blanchot). Coprophagia can only reincorporate the fallen turd into the entire digestive process in the mode of an endless repetition ("the monotony which results from this sort of abuse"). The turd digested comes out turd, leaving nothing behind. The process of negation that the body operates on food in which food is negated dialectically (that is, retained and sublated) draws nothing from the turd. The turd will not be *aufgehoben*.

Although "La Raison de Sade," Blanchot's second article on Sade, is Hegelian, Blanchot's third text on Sade would go beyond the Hegelian closure and even looks back and classifies the earlier dialectical reading of Sade from without. In that third article, "L'Inconvenance majeure" ("The Major Impropriety"), Blanchot writes that there are three ways in which Sade's work explores the excessive nature of reason, three different faces by which reason's energetic process manifests itself. "One is of an encyclopedic

nature. It's a question of recording all human possibilities."[15] As we have seen, the gratuitous stubborn-
ness of coprophagia in *120 Journées* undermines this
encyclopedic project. The second face of Sade's reason is dialectic. Yet again the turd or corpse comes to
parody and undercut "the supposition . . . of basing
the rational sovereignty of man upon a transcendent
power of negation" (*L'Entretien*, p. 327). Finally, reason in Sade "seeks itself through the movement of
writing" (p. 327). The incessant impulsion to write is
the insistence of that which exceeds any dialectic,
the attempt of that excess or waste to reincorporate
itself into the dialectic. (Coprophagia is the parodic
representation of this endless repetition of the effort:
aufheben the dead turd.) This "writing mania,"
infinite repetition, "eternal resifting," is for Blanchot
Sade's *inconvenance majeure*: impropriety in the
major mode.

The mere name Sade is sufficient to evoke notions of impropriety and scandal. Blanchot's original-
ity as a reader of Sade is to distinguish between a
major and a minor mode of impropriety. The title
"L'Inconvenance majeure" is changed, when the article is published in *L'Entretien infini*, to "L'Insurrection, la folie d'écrire" ("Insurrection, writing
mania"). *Inconvenance* in the major mode is Sade's
interminable, excessive writing, not the perverse,
crude, improper episodes he describes. Although the
third of Blanchot's articles on Sade is specifically
devoted to the *folie d'écrire*, his notion of a more
radical scandal pervades his reading from the first. In
"Quelques remarques sur Sade" he writes: "What
[Sade] writes and what is supposed to constitute a
real book, an author's book, drags him along in a
terrible movement without end, where literary re-

sources, language's proprieties, founder" (pp. 242–
43). Sade is a perverse writer not because he
writes about perversions, but because his writing
itself is perverse.

"The discomfort caused by reading Sade is not
due to the singular adventures he recounts to us"
(ibid., p. 243). The reader is not disturbed (euphemism for arousal as or by violation) by the particular
acts in Sade's novels. It is the general movement of
Sadian writing which creates the "discomfort." Here
we find the same structure as Blanchot's reading of
the Sadian libertine as not aroused by any particular
destruction, as moved only by a universal negation:
"all the particular cruelties are now merely destined
to verify and confirm this universal annihilation"
(ibid., p. 246). The particular act, the moment which
outside the incessant process is but a lifeless turd, is
Sade in the minor mode. Any perverse act within the
Sadian text is already sublated by a movement in
itself so perverse that any particular manifestation,
however outrageous, is appropriate within it. The
individual "scandalous" acts are tame scandal, scandal *in the family* (in the comfort of good company),
inasmuch as they belong in a text that is supposed to
be universally scandalous. How can the improper
maintain its impropriety there where it is in its
place? Scandal retains its violent force by reasserting
itself in a writing that exceeds and decays any circumscription, whether positivistically encyclopedic
or dialectical. The shit in coprophagia reassumes its
all-pervasive stink by what Lély calls its "monstrously exaggerated place."

Blanchot views any particular episode of the
Sadian text as the domesticated representation of a
scandal so radical that *any* representation of it is

already short of that irretrievability. Thus any perverse act, any specific transgression, far from being a
cause for discomfort, partakes of the side of Sade that
is most *propre,* most comfortable, most pleasurable.
Blanchot can say of Sade, "His demon is not that of
lubricity. It is more dangerous. It is . . . the writing
mania, infinite, interminable, incessant, movement"
(*L'Entretien,* p. 341). Sex and violence is Sade in the
minor mode; the violence and desire of writing is
major mode, absolutely inappropriable impropriety.
We can co-opt and use scandal *(inconvenance)* in the
minor mode to add piquancy to our pleasures. This
would be the corpse that the murderer *could simply*
use to enjoy his feeling of mastery: recoverable death,
appropriate impropriety.

According to Blanchot, "Henceforth all the particular cruelties are now merely destined to verify
and confirm this universal annihilation, to bring to
the Unique One [the sovereign libertine] the agreeable proofs of his overabundant existence in the
midst of nothing" ("Remarques," p. 246). The secondary act of verification and confirmation is thus
agreeable, pleasant: the domestic side of sex, comfortable violence. The incessant, insatiable craving
for negation (the progress of the *Aufhebung*) frees the
libertine from any discomfort concerning his individual acts. Like Hegel's philosopher who (from the
standpoint of absolute knowledge) can experience
and watch the individual moments of the *Phenomenology* (with all their pain and struggle) as pleasing
proofs of what he already knows, the libertine can
get some simple pleasure, in the minor mode.

In "La Raison de Sade," however, Blanchot's reiteration of the fact that any particular destruction is
simply a verification of the universal nothingness

undergoes a curious transformation: "The sadistic man seems surprisingly free in relation to his victims . . . that is because the violence, in them, is aiming for something else than them, goes well beyond them, and merely verifies frenetically, endlessly, in each particular case, the general act of destruction" (*L&S*, p. 34). The verification which, in "Remarques," is articulated as "agreeable" here becomes "frenetic" and insatiable. As Blanchot systematizes the dialectical structure of an infinite negation sublating any individual moments (the main difference between the contemporaneous "Quelques remarques sur Sade" and "La Raison de Sade" is the systematization reflected in the degree of formality of the titles), the impatient violence of that negation ("too great a hatred for any of its objects to matter," *L&S*, p. 39) becomes intrinsic to each moment. As a true Hegelian dialectical progress, the necessity of the *Aufhebung* is structurally inscribed into each moment. The overabundant multiplicity of specific crimes—which at some point serves Blanchot as proof of the agreeable insignificance of each "verification"—can now be recognized as symptomatic of the libertine's displeasureable, itching insatiability. From such a perspective the very movement of the dialectic, in its smooth and constant progress, can be seen as an all-too-tame attempt to contain the infinite restlessness of Sade.

In "L'Inconvenance majeure," the dialectical process which dominates "La Raison de Sade" is put in its place as a less radical manifestation of *la folie d'écrire*—Sade's major impropriety, the necessity of saying everything. Juliette's last words in *Juliette* are "Philosophy should say everything" (9:586). This, for Blanchot, is Sade at his most scandalous, his least recoverable: "the 'everything' which is at stake . . . is no longer only the universality of encyclopedic knowledge . . . nor even the totality of an experience where meaning is achieved through the movement of a negation pushed to its end—a circular discourse which is thus the affirmation—closed and complete—of mastery of everything" (*L'Entretien*, p. 328). Sade's Hegelianism (as original and anachronistic as such a notion might be) takes its place next to Sade's Enlightenment encyclopedianism within the minor mode: Sade *propre*, "closed and complete."

La folie d'écrire, Sade's incessant attempt to say everything, can be expressed as his passion to say what isn't said. This phrase can be read according to a euphemistic or an absolute interpretation, pointing to the distinction between minor and major impropriety. The locution "what isn't said" normally means that which contingently cannot be said, that which is not right to say in polite company: that which is not said, *in the family*. To say "what isn't said" is to scandalize, to create a stink somewhere. The radical sense of "what isn't said" is that which absolutely cannot be said, that which exceeds language, that which renders the philosophical obligation or compulsion to say everything a futile, eternal attempt to appropriate the inappropriable.

The tame, euphemistic sense of "what isn't said" allows Blanchot to reinstate a simple, pleasant aspect of Sade. "And Sade can certainly experience pleasure, a simple and salubrious pleasure, in the strong scenes that he imagines . . . where he says what isn't said" (ibid). Sadian scandal in-the-minor-mode includes not just episodes of action ("agreeable proofs") but a domesticated version of language-as-

scandal. Sade's crude, blasphemous, "improper" language is the parodic version of the major impropriety
that is his passion to say everything, to say that
which "is not said." Blanchot would have it that this
minor mode of improper language is free from any
discomfort—"a simple and salubrious pleasure." The
contingent mode (sex and violence) is healthy; the
absolute mode (writing), *folie*. Blanchot has discovered comfortable violence, impropriety in the family,
salubricity.[16] ("Sade's demon is not lubricity.")

The first two versions of Justine's story[17] can be
placed under the aegis of the attempt in-the-minor-
mode to say what isn't said. The dynamic of Justine's
narration of her own story is her effort to "paint"
(Justine's word) her scandalous activities in language
respectful of propriety. "I am softening the expressions, you understand; in the same way, madame, I
will weaken the descriptions. Alas, their hue is so
obscene that your modesty would suffer from their
nudity at least as much as would my timidity" (3:83).
In the domain of *Justine*, there is something potentially sayable, a tangible naked body, that is not said,
but is veiled behind what is said. What isn't said,
here, is that which would violate contingent social
propriety, but is nonetheless perfectly respectful of
language, just not of the language that is *propre* to
Justine. The narrator substitutes good words for bad
words. There are "descriptions" and "expressions,"
given in her experience, which she will veil and
euphemize out of respect for "that which one does
not say." In this context, it seems that all that would
be necessary in order to say everything (as Juliette
says philosophy should) is to lift the veils, call things
by their proper name, defy convention, violate propriety. So, in the third version of Justine's story *(La*

Nouvelle Justine and *Juliette*), Justine is silent and Juliette (Justine's own improper sister) becomes a narrator.

The narration, which in the first two versions was pleasant and agreeable, becomes, in *La Nouvelle Justine* and *Juliette,* infinitely frenetic. The 1797 version of the two sisters' story is some thirty-six hundred pages long. "There, the simply repetitive force bears the major impropriety, that of a narration that encounters no *interdit* [prohibition; what isn't said—minor mode], because there is no other (this entire limit-work tells us with the monotony of its frightening clamor) than the time of *l'entre-dire* [between statements; what isn't said—major mode], that pure stop that can only be reached by never ceasing to speak" (*L'Entretien,* pp. 328–29). *Juliette* ends with the heroine saying, "Why then be afraid to make it public. . . . Philosophy must say everything" (9:586), as if the very book we were reading were the triumph of the effort to say everything. Yet that triumph of circumscription (of making *Juliette* belong to Juliette) is undercut by a final paragraph in which the other narrator (outside of and encompassing Juliette) tells the reader that "this woman . . . having died without writing the final events of her life, *absolutely* deprives *any writer* of the possibility of showing it to the public" (ibid., p. 587, my italics). The derision of Juliette's successful saying of what isn't said (minor mode) opens onto the horizon of that which is exterior to the text. The following sentence, the last sentence in this gigantic novel, is a diatribe against those who would try to fill in this final blank in the story: "Those who would wish to undertake it would only be offering us their reveries in place of realities, which would make an astonishing difference in the eyes of people of taste, and particularly of those who took some interest in the reading of this work." The unspecific multiplicity of "those who would wish" (as if the compulsion to write *this* book were shared by everyone) corresponds to the endless proliferation of attempts ("simply repetitive force") playing out the passion to reach "this pure stop." The narrator would harshly sever the fantasmatic potentialities for fulfillment ("reveries"). The monstrous opus can only end through the assumption of the impossibility of its own task ("say everything").

The inevitable progression towards major scandal, the opening onto absolute exteriority, is necessarily inscribed into the effort to say that which is not said (euphemistic sense), that which respectable people do not say. Once the propriety, under which Justine labors, is called into question, a passage to the limit will reduce to nothing every particular *interdit*, for they are but pale images of the radical "time of *l'entre-dire*." Just as in the Sadian world the strip-tease gives way to a more radical stripping away of the flesh (laceration and dismemberment), so too does the attempt to reveal the "nudity" that Justine would veil lead only to the realization that the naked word is no more final truth than the veiled euphemism. The gradual process of possession or revelation in Sade leads, not to the naked body, but to "a work strewn with corpses" ("link[s] between here and nowhere"). The onward progress of the passion to say what isn't said leads, not to the naked, crude word, but to "that pure stop that can only be reached by never ceasing to speak"—silence as infinite repetition, coprophagia.

For Blanchot, the epic of 1797 (*La Nouvelle Justine suivie de l'histoire de Juliette*) is a far more

radical book than *Justine*. They are the same statement, but *Justine* is made in-the-minor-mode,
whereas the latter version writes this statement in-
the-major-mode. The very bulk of the 1797 work constitutes an unreadability far surpassing any negative
reaction to the sex and violence contained within.
Not only does Justine as narrator obey the rules of
polite language, but the earlier novel in its manage-
able size poses no outrage to appropriable literature.
Blanchot calls *Justine* "a rather coarse story" (*L&S*, p.
28) in which the affirmation that virtue's reward is
misfortune while vice reaps prosperity "seems a simple factitious story that, in the guise of proofs, is
illustrated by the arrangement of a story whose author is master" (ibid., p. 24). Blanchot's minor mode,
whether it be Hegelian circumscription ("the affirmation, closed and complete, of mastery of
everything"), the particular acts of cruelty ("bring to
the Unique One the agreeable proofs of his overabundant existence"), or the novel *Justine* ("a story whose
author is master"), is always the register where mastery is possible.

The two sisters (Blanchot points out, *L&S*, p. 28)
actually traverse the same experiences: Justine, in-
the-minor-mode; Juliette, in-the-major-mode. Juliette
is everything that is not *propre*. Not only is she not
proper, correct, nor clean, but she is not selfsame.
Justine, the virtuous sister, remains stubbornly the
same throughout her adventures. Near the end of
Justine, the heroine is compared to a technical virgin:
"The latter [the virgin] has her physical and moral
virtue, the former [Justine] has only the virtue of
feelings; but it is part of her existence and nowhere
will you find a creature more replete with candor
and honesty" (3:308). Justine is noncontingently

proper: no event is sufficient to violate her integrity, her identity, her propriety. Although constantly harassed by impropriety in-the-minor-mode, radical violence (the destruction of identity) appears not to touch Justine. Juliette, on the contrary, is the whore: constant metamorphosis as reflection of others' desires. Juliette's propriety, her identity, cannot be violated because her desire is explicitly the other's desire. Her sovereignty is her refusal of self-mastery, her refusal of self.

Justine's path is Hegelian as she elicits her antithesis (provokes her violation) and passes on to her next confrontation, at once having been violated and maintaining her integrity. Justine is raped dialectically: that is, her virginity (integrity, wholeness) is destroyed and nonetheless remains (*aufgehoben*). Juliette's absolute prostitution erodes and derides the circumscriptive mastery (the subject's standpoint of absolute knowledge) of the dialectic, for it disrupts the possibility of continuity between moments.

Juliette declares: "My lubricity, always modeled after men's whims, never is lit except by the fire of their passions; I am only really inflamed by their desires, and the only sensual pleasure I know is that of satisfying all their deviations" (9:86). Juliette as woman (whore / slave) passes through her story with no particular tastes or perversions of her own, always open to the imprint of her friends' tastes. Juliette's peculiar devotion to her friends consists in being in perfect harmony with them, until she responds to the desires of another friend—going through a total metamorphosis. She never betrays a friend gratuitously; she always betrays one friend for another (Mme de Donis for Sbrigani, Clairwil for Durand). It is not a betrayal of a friend, for the betrayed is no longer a friend. Juliette merely responds to the wishes of whomever she enters into conjuncture with. The total floozie, Juliette is not concerned with consistency. The whore's charm lies in her ability to appear to treat the other as a unique exception. Juliette confides to her *best friend* Clairwil (whom she eventually poisons): "Nothing bothers me as much as these preferences. You are the only one, my angel, the only one in the world, whom I pardon for loving me" (*Juliette,* 9:412). The absolute flattery of making an exception to one's dislike for exceptions is irresistible. Indifferent to her reputation, the whore can flaunt her contradictions, counting upon her charm, not her clarity and logic, to persuade.

Justine, on the other hand, always goes off alone: her comings and goings are always responses to her own wishes. Juliette is not her own woman (a woman as woman is never her own); she is absolutely improper, not *propre* to herself. The ending of her book, where the narrator warns against those who would fill in her story, opens up onto Juliette's lack of status as absolute whore. Her story could be anyone's; it would merely reflect the desires of any writer that chose to model her, "offering us their reveries in place of realities" ("always modeled after men's whims"). Her story would be absolutely not her own; its potential multiplicity of endings is her complete lack of self-identity. The "reality" of the whore (woman) is inseparable from the "reveries" of men. Juliette attains to the apotheosis of perversion by having absolutely no desires of her own. She is absolutely inappropriable by being totally available and positively inconstant. Juliette's strength is her complete lack of resistance.

In Sade the whore is also the storyteller. In *120 Journées* the four storytellers are experienced prostitutes who by this role escape the life and death consequences of the master / victim confrontation, who survive by being aggressively, scandalously at the disposal of the master's whim, being interpreters of that whim. Julie, the one victim who survives, does so by passing into the ranks of the whores.[18] Julie passes from being Justine (victim) to being Juliette (whore). It is as whore / storyteller / woman that the philosopher can take on the task of saying everything. The slut is scandalous in-the-major-mode, not because she is wanton and sexual, but because she bears the inscription of the other's desires. She is absolutely inconstant, as each inscription is erased to make room for the next, as each friend is killed according to the next friend's wishes.

Blanchot writes that the major violation felt by a reader of Sade stems from the fact that his writing is at once absolutely clear and absolutely obscure (*L'Entretien*, p. 325). "The result is that everything which is said is clear, but seems at the mercy of something which has not been said, that a bit later what was not allowed to be said, shows itself and is recovered by logic, but it in turn obeys the movement of a still hidden force, and that in the end, everything is brought to light, everything gains expression, but everything is also plunged again into obscurity" (*L&S*, p. 19). Everything that is said is said as if by a whore, who speaks "at the mercy" of someone who does not speak (situation of *120 Journées*). That which is said in Sade's writing mania is like Juliette's lubricity, which is "always modeled after men's

whims, never is lit except by the fire of their passions." The expression of Sade's thought plays the
peculiar game of the hussy, whose brazen flirtation
consists, not in veiling and resisting, but in giving
everything you want until you have all you have
asked for and yet she is still there, other and resistant
just by being other. The radical movement of Sade's
writing as whorish flirtation exposes the noncontin-
gency of resistance, reveals the ultimate irretrievability of the available, the obscurity in that which is
absolutely clear, the taunting metaphoricity of even
the most naked word. The whore,[19] in her absolute
availability, teaches the same lesson as the friend in-
the-major-mode about respect for the radically irreducible distance. The prostitute does everything (the
storyteller, Sade, says everything), yet each of her
acts (stories) reveals nothing about her. She does not
give "herself" to us, for she is always a reference to
something else. The whore is here and nowhere at
all, for when you have her, you have that which is
not self-identical (woman-as-woman is never her
own woman, always the reveries of men). The floozie
is precisely the "corpse's presence" which is totally
at your disposal, and yet always exceeds you ("a
relation to the unknown").

Of course, if the storyteller is a whore, then Justine's propriety is somewhat compromised. Justine,
as she tells her own story, loses her selfsameness.
She splits into Justine and Thérèse. Is this then lack
of self-identity in-the-minor-mode? Just as Justine
uses euphemistic words in the place of other, "improper" words, so she substitutes the name Thérèse
for the name Justine. In this nonviolent form of metaphoricity, there is something solid to stop the play of
substitution: an original name and an alias—a clear,

unidirectional distinction between the original and the substitute. Yet this nonthreatening lack of self-sameness points to the more radical prostitution of Juliette.

Justine tells her story because Mme de Lorsange [Juliette's married name] and her lover M. de Corville desire to hear it: "Mme de Lorsange . . . in a low voice manifested to M. de Corville the wish she had to learn directly from the mouth of this girl herself the story of her misfortunes, and M. de Cor-ville . . . also was conceiving the same desire" (*Justine*, 3:66). Justine protests that it would be "a sort of revolt against [God's] sacred designs. . . . I don't dare" (ibid.). Yet Justine gives in to their caprice and goes on to tell her story with style and relish, "inflamed by their desires," as it were. *Justine*, in fact, escapes from being "a rather coarse story" through the heroine's equivocal position as narrator. The discomfort, which Blanchot considers to be the effect of the repetitive monotony and the whorish play (saying everything yet still offering resistance) of the 1797 epic, is already provoked in the two earlier versions by a certain perverse, nonutilitarian desire to please (to pander to the other's desire) in Justine-as-narrator: "If my cruel situation would allow me to amuse you for a moment, madame, when I ought only to be thinking of softening your heart" (3:74).

The daily session of perversions in *120 Journées* begins first with the prostitute as storyteller recounting several acts of perversion, whereupon the masters, inspired by these examples, enact similar passions upon the victims. Every time Justine meets someone, she tells the tale of her woes (recounts several acts of perversion), whereupon she is aston-

ished to find that the interlocutor reacts by being
inspired to actualize similar perversions with her as
victim. As she ends her story, her listeners are
tempted to finish it off according to their reveries,
just as the narrator of *Juliette* feared that "those who
would wish" would continue Juliette's story, thus
violating her integrity (the integrity the narrator
would attribute to one "true" Juliette with her own
story in his gallant effort to make an "honest woman"
of her). Justine as narrator is tainted with a whorish
complicity that necessitates her split into Justine
(standpoint of absolute knowledge) and Thérèse (naive consciousness taking the struggle of each moment seriously, blind to reason's ruse). Ultimately,
the roles must be reapportioned so that Juliette (the
previous interlocutor) becomes narrator, Justine becomes silent victim, and Thérèse disappears. Justine's veiled complicity in Thérèse's violations leads,
of necessity (the necessity of saying everything), to
the revelation of that complicity, which, once uncovered (since exposed complicity is scandal), must belong to Juliette, the scandalous sister.

Given this shift in our perspective, Juliette as
narrator of her own story is responding to her own
desire, whereas Justine is fulfilling the other's desire.[20] Juliette, who can proudly claim her successfully radical impropriety, can frame it into story
form, is her own whore (woman), whereas Justine
slips away from her own grasp by compromising her
self-mastery, by responding to a perverse compulsion
to tell her story *in detail.*

Justine's perversion inhabits the details. What
Blanchot dismisses (salubricity ? *sale* [dirty] lubricity) as the "cruel vicissitudes . . . which more likely
serve to amuse us" (*L'Entretien*, p. 325) are in their

very capacity as mere diversion, as gratuitous frills, that which is most perverse: pure waste, turds. Justine explains to Mme de Lorsange (Juliette as Justine's interlocutor, as locus of emission of the desire that causes Justine to speak) "that it . . . is very difficult to detain you with amusing details before conversing with you about my misfortune" (Justine, 3:74). Justine does nonetheless proffer these amusing details on her own without being asked, yet displays her embarrassed desire to fulfill the other's desire to be amused by saying she really should not waste her time with such things. In fact, Justine as narrator is constantly recounting minute details. She gives everyone's age, describes every room in detail, lists the menu for every meal. Justine's narration exposes the fact that what is most outrageous about the philosophical obligation or compulsion to say everything is that it plays itself out as an incessant attempt, linked to an inability, to sublate (aufheben) the details (coprophagia). The simple, agreeable verification reveals itself as infinitely frenetic.

Justine, in her effort at circumscriptive mastery, lists the age of everyone she encounters. Yet unlike the monks at Sainte-Marie-des-Bois she never completes the categorization. The numbers are so many corpses studding the text: dead moments cut off from the dialectical progress. They should be absolutely appropriable (addable, subtractable, multipliable, divisible), but they are the derision, in their brute contingency, of the project to say everything. The obligation to say all, coupled with lucidity to the correlative necessity for absolutely interminable talking, leads in the Sadian text to a movement of systematization that is always either short of or beyond any closed system.

Whenever one of Justine's libertine interlocutors asks her to repeat certain details,[21] he is manifesting his libidinal interest, his perverse status as listener. It is the insignificant details in their multiplicity that normally constitute what isn't said. A prinicipal rule of social propriety is not to bore with an excess of irrelevant details.[22] As Justine is telling of her adventure with the counterfeiter, she says, "He handles all my parts which modesty forbids naming" (3:271). Improper language fractures the wholeness of the collective, all-encompassing "all my parts" into multiple details—wild and inappropriable in their diversity. Modesty, respect for propriety, consists in presenting what isn't said as an appropriable whole, which as such would pose no real threat to the subject's mastery: "the affirmation, closed and complete, of mastery of everything." The major scandal of Sade's tearing aside the veil of modesty is the revelation that there is not just one, central, hidden end-of-the-line there (strip-tease as progression to *Le Sexe*), but a multiplicity of parts: "a work strewn with corpses." The deadly unassimilability of the plethora of details is lived as boredom. In a rare instance of editing, Justine says, "If you like, madame, . . . I'm going to limit myself to explaining here the abbreviated story of the first month I spent in this convent, that is to say the principal anecdotes of this period; the rest would be a repetition: the monotony of this stay would spread to my accounts" (3:193). "The principal anecdotes" recalls Lély's "principal perversions" (see p. 46 above). Lély complains that Sade would "graft" coprophagia onto the significant, central perversions, which would therefore be *déchus*, wasted. In such a manner Justine's compulsive inclusion of irrelevant details contaminates the principal anecdotes, those with redeeming social worth.

Justine, the minor-mode statement, is thus not merely agreeable proof (verification and confirmation) of "a simple factitious thesis," not a mere pleasant actualization of the author's mastery. *Justine* stinks through and through from the out-of-place, unassimilable details. The earlier, shorter novel is already an evocation of the major impropriety of the longer opus, already the work of the insatiable restlessness that necessitates eternal talking in order to be still. The reader does not escape discomfort in reading the earlier versions, for Sade's impropriety is major precisely because it appears where it does not belong, where it is least expected, in the context of that which is most tame, death and violation *in the family* (incest). The major impropriety is that ultimate exteriority that is nonetheless interior to the relation between the most intimate friends.

3 | Whoring among Friends: Klossowski on Sade

> It is extraordinary how a woman quickly adopts the principles of him who fucks her.
> —La Dubois in *La Nouvelle Justine* (6:154)

In 1947, Bataille published "Le Secret de Sade,"[1] which is billed as a review of (1) a new editon of *120 Journées de Sodome,* (2) an edition of *Les Infortunes de la vertu* with an introduction by Jean Paulhan, and (3) Pierre Klossowski's *Sade mon prochain.* Although frequently quoting from Jean Paulhan, this "review" quotes directly from Klossowski's book only twice. And the second quotation (p. 304) merely repeats a couple of phrases from the first passage quoted. The unique passage chosen to be included is taken from neither of the two Klossowski essays which Bataille explicitly names and discusses. Rather, Bataille quotes from the third chapter of *Sade mon prochain*—"Sous le masque de l'athéisme"[2]—a study he neither names nor discusses. Bataille uses this quotation twice to illustrate his own argument that Sade meditates in a manner analogous to reli-

gious devotion upon the object of his desire. At one
point Bataille takes exception to what is being said
in the Klossowski passage quoted. Following the
clause "the romantic soul which is merely a nostalgic
state of faith" (Klossowski found in Bataille) is a
footnote which reads, "I obviously cannot follow
Klossowski in this reservation" (p. 157). "Nostalgic
state of faith" (thus put into relief by Bataille), when
replaced into the context of the 1947 edition of *Sade
mon prochain*, alludes to the final article of the book,
"Le Corps du néant," never mentioned by Bataille, subtitled "The Experience of the Death of
God in Nietzsche and the *Nostalgia* for an Authentic
Experience in *Georges Bataille*" (my italics). The
main line of argumentation in that article could be
summarized briefly as "Georges Bataille is merely a
nostalgic state of faith."

Sade is discussed at some length in this article
on Nietzsche and, Bataille, justifying perhaps its appearance in the book. However at least one reader
believes he has found the "real" explanation of this
inclusion. Aimé Patri[3] continues Klossowski's gesture of removing various of Sade's masks (which
itself is an extension of Sade's unmasking the various
institutions of his time) by positing Bataille as the
true face behind the figure Sade in *Sade mon prochain*. Patri finds it a "peculiar idea" to try to harrow
hell and rescue Sade, who has been there all these
years. Such an extravagance would be unthinkable;
therefore Klossowski must be up to something else.
Patri has solved this *étude à clef*: "The last chapter of
the book finally makes us understand that, when we
heard about Sade, in reality, it was about Georges
Bataille, who is still alive, and whose friend wished
to save him, although he wildly resists."

Klossowski's unmasking of Sade ("Sous le masque de l'athéisme"—"Under the Mask of Atheism") is a more interesting and equivocal process than Patri's hermeneutic detective work. Patri gestures towards dismissal (sending away, sending back to its proper place that which has been discovered sneaking in under false pretenses): the book is a private communication—from one friend to another—posing as a public work. Yet the very move towards dismissal (digestion by assimilating the dead Sade to the living Bataille) spins out an unassimilable "kernel of truth." Not that, through a unidirectional reduction, we must see Bataille as the real face ("in reality") behind the mask Sade; but that somehow a whirl of masks and texts has been set in motion. The names and texts Sade, Bataille, Nietzsche, and Klossowski are caught up in a dance which, rather than being simply attributable to the friendship between Bataille and Klossowski (the fact outside the text, "in reality," which would condition the text), is itself implicated in the constitution of such a friendship—an unabashedly textual friendship.

Klossowski takes notice of Patri's detective work in a context which opens up the one-for-one substitution into a dizzying identificatory free-for-all. In "De l'opportunité à étudier l'oeuvre du marquis de Sade," Klossowski writes: "My unbelieving friends confuse the case of Sade with the crisis of the generation which followed him and even worse, with their own crisis."[4] First confusion: Klossowski's atheist friends (Bataille carefully reminds us, on both occasions of quoting, that this is "Klossowski the Christian" to whom he is referring) confuse the generations following Sade—and even worse, themselves—with Sade. "They do not realize that Sade escapes them as

soon as they take him at his word, whereas they do
not escape from Sade: they become his characters—
more or less successfully." The distinction text / exterior has been turned inside-out. The readers who
think they know who Sade is, who think they are
Sade, become Sade's characters.

"*On veut se servir de Sade* . . . *pour s'expliquer*
[they want to use Sade to explain themselves]," Klossowski writes, still referring to his atheist friends. At
this point, flush in the middle of a field of mistaken
identification, Klossowski injects the following footnote: "And thus it was written that I had used Sade
[*Et ainsi on a écrit que je m'étais servi de Sade*] to
make confession, to act upon my intimates, and that
pursuing a discussion with Georges Bataille, I supposedly, in the form of my book, addressed an exhor-
tation to him, all the while pretending to speak of
Sade." Neither a disavowal of Patri's accusation nor
an admission of guilt, this invocation of Patri, in the
margins of what might appear to be an accusation of
his unbelieving friends upon the same grounds, contaminates the confrontation Patri-Klossowski with
the same beyond-right-and-wrong complicity as
holds between Klossowski and his friends. The "on"
of "on a écrit" immediately recalls "on" of "on veut
se servir," so that Patri (the referent of "on a écrit")
seems to join the ranks of the unbelieving friends
who try to use Sade to make their own points. It thus
might seem that Klossowski is adding this note to
dismiss his adversary Patri in the wake of his principal effort against unbelievers in general.

Yet the note goes on to set up an analogy, not
between Patri and the unbelievers, but between Klossowski and his atheist friends (and to correlatively
identify Patri and Klossowski as righters of wrong

identifications). Patri accuses Klossowski of the same crime as Klossowski attributes to the unbelievers. "Je m'étais servi de Sade" echoes "on veut se servir de Sade." The surprising analogy which plays itself out against the backdrop of the expected opposite equivalence (Patri = unbelievers) partakes of the same gesture which allows this Christian to speak of "my unbelieving friends." The word "friends" here cuts across the opposition Christian / unbeliever, contaminating the purity of that duality.

The interplay between footnote and text causes a splitting of Klossowski into Klossowski the accuser (= Patri) and Klossowski the guilty (= unbelieving friends). This split finds its analogue within the Sadian text in Justine's split into Justine and Thérèse (or Justine and Sophie in Les Infortunes de la vertu) in response to the encounter with Juliette that takes place in the margins of Justine's story proper. Entering into a pact with her unbelieving sister (the pact to tell the story Juliette wishes to hear), Justine splits into the perverse, guilty storyteller (identification with Juliette, elsewhere a monstrous libertine) and Thérèse the innocent victim (accuser of the likes of Juliette). In trying to talk of Sade, Klossowski has (as he predicted) become a Sadian character.

The article continues: "Undoubtedly Sade, I would say, is the first one responsible for this quid pro quo." It is impossible to tell which quid pro quo is "this quid pro quo." The really frightening quid pro quo undercuts the very possibility of keeping track of the quid and the quo, of keeping their "original" identities straight. Sade, "the first one responsible," is thus the originator, the author, of this vertiginous substitution.

Klossowski begins this article by confronting the arguments of "my unbelieving friends"; later (p. 719) he directs his response to "the grumblings of my Christian friends." Like one of Sade's philosophical heroes, Klossowski is warmed to discourse in the comfort of good company, inspired by friendly differences of opinion. Describing the conversation at a dinner party for three outrageous libertines (great friends), Juliette says that one of them (Noirceuil) "only controverted so as better to make his friends shine" (*Juliette*, 8:207).

Noirceuil turns against (*contra-vertere*) his friends in order to arouse them, rubbing against them, rubbing them the wrong way, to make them shine. Argumentative resistance, like its sexual analogue modesty, is a libertine refinement, adding spice to pleasure. "The origin of modesty was . . . merely a lustful refinement: people were very willing to desire for a longer time so as to be more excited, and then fools took for a virtue what was simply an artificial refinement of libertinage" (*Juliette*, 8:70–71). As a libertine affectation, sexual resistance is founded upon a complicity between resister and resisted to prolong the fiction (of noncomplicity) so as to prolong the friction. Friendship, rather than leading to the dissolution of all pretenses in naked frankness, makes possible a masked ball of titillating artificed resistance.

Klossowski, as mask, as locus of emission of the 1947 article "De l'opportunité . . . ," is thus constituted as the point of intersection between his atheist friends and his Christian friends. This is not a timeless identity; neither are these friendships eternal. In 1970, in an introduction to a Klossowski bibliography for *l'Arc*, René Micha writes: "In the strictest terms, [Klossowski] only recognized as 'his' the texts which appeared after 1954."⁵ Noirceuil, who outdid himself in order to make his friends shine, will later kill Saint-Fond, one of the guests at this very dinner party. This textual friendship is not productive of eternal fidelity and intimacy. Rather it is a conjuncture, the glorious production of an instant in which friends join efforts to achieve brilliance.

Nietzsche calls such a radiant conjuncture star friendship. "We are two ships each of which has its goal and course; our paths may cross and we may celebrate a feast together, as we did. . . . But then the almighty force of our tasks drove us apart again into different seas and sunny zones, and perhaps we shall never see each other again. . . . Let us then *believe* in our star friendship even if we should be compelled to be earth enemies."⁶ Friends in Sade's books come together with great warmth and share in extravagant good times ("celebrate a feast together"), yet cannot be depended upon not to betray or even kill each other in a later episode, under the sign of a different constellation of forces. This lack of fidelity is not a proof of the characters' essential solitude, but rather of a wilder friendship—star friendship.

Star friendship is textual. It does not endure, yet leaves traces of its radiant configurations. Such friendship is *textus*, a woven thing, a point of crossing of separate strands. The intersection of Nietzsche and Sade (star friendship) returns us to the meeting-place of those two friends: Klossowski and Bataille. Klossowski's article on Nietzsche and Bataille ("Le Corps du néant") in *Sade mon prochain* does not survive the shift in constellations governing the 1967 reedition of the book. In a letter included in the introduction to the *Arc* bibliography, Klossowski dis-

misses that piece, condemning what he calls his former "acephalizing tergiversations in regard to Bataille." In "Le Corps du néant" Klossowski builds an
argument upon Bataille's claim to be acephalous,
relating the headless state to the impossibility of
communication, and, beyond that, of authentic experience. In the period before World War II Bataille
headed the journal *Acéphale,* to which Klossowski
was a frequent contributor. "Le Corps du néant" was
originally given as a lecture at the Dominican convent of Saint-Maximin. The scene of "Le Corps du
néant": a discussion by Klossowski about his atheist
friend Georges Bataille in the company of his Christian friends. In this context Klossowski perpetrates
tergiversations.

According to *Le Petit Robert,* "tergiverser"
means "use detours, evasions, to avoid giving a clear
answer, to retard the moment of decision." Tergiversation, thus, has the same function as modesty in the
libertine context: "a lustful refinement: people were
very willing to desire for a longer time so as to be
more excited." The tergiversator seductively leads
the suitor on, avoiding a yes-or-no answer to the
proposition, prolonging the itching doubt. Klossowski's tergiversations in regard to his friend Bataille recall Noirceuil, who "only controverted so as
better to make his friends shine." "Controverser"
(turn against) is closely akin to "tergiverser" *(tergum-
vertere,* turn one's back). The physical image is more
striking in "tergiverser," making explicit the fact that
the positive concomitant to the act of turning away
is the exposure of the back. *Tergum,* the Latin word
for back, has made its highly sexual entry into the
domain of modern French and English in the expression "coit(us) à tergo"—intercourse from behind.

Klossowski in his flirtatious resistance to Bataille is offering his friend his behind.

The two friends engage ("as it were") in what Klossowski (in "Le Philosophe scélérat") finds to be the central Sadian libertine act, sodomy. Sodomy could be considered a tergiversation inasmuch as the anus would be a detour in relation to the "normal" central sexual goal—penetration of the vagina. The "proper" place for sexual tergiversation is foreplay. In that context, perverse sexual play is teleologically subordinate to *the* sexual goal—vagino-penile intercourse. That act is constituted as *telos* through an anticipation of its consequences—that is, pregnancy. In *La Philosophie dans le boudoir,* Eugénie asks her instructors for guidance in how to avoid those very consequences. Mme de Saint-Ange replies: "A girl never exposes herself to having babies except inasmuch as she lets it be put in her cunt. Let her *avoid with care* this mode of pleasure; let her indiscriminately *offer in its place* her hand, her mouth, her tits, or her asshole" (3:413, my italics). The lesson is clear—tergiversate ("use detours").

Mme de Saint-Ange goes on to distinguish the last of these sexual detours from the others. "With this last path, she will get much pleasure, even much more than elsewhere; with the other ways, she will give it." Ass-fucking, unlike the other evasions, is the parodic revelation of the resister's complicity. The girl who wishes to guard her honor turns her back upon the aggressor, offering her behind, but ultimately gives away her complicity by the great pleasure this tergiversation affords her.

A truly subversive *(sub-vertere,* turn upsidedown) tergiversation, the offer of the anus not only delays the "moment of truth" (penetration of the va-

gina by the penis, the "true" goal of sexual activity),
but makes that moment unnecessary, even impossible. The penis spends itself in the anus. The asshole
usurps the cunt's position. The tergiversation suc-
ceeds; the girl "avoids giving a clear answer" and
thus keeps her technical virginity. Perversity is no
longer merely in the service of "normal" sexuality.

The same story is told twice in the collection of
Sade's short stories, *Historiettes, contes et fabliaux.*
"L'Epoux complaisant," the name given to the short-
est version of this magnetic little tale, serves in one
edition as the title for the entire collection.[7] In that
story and in "Soit fait ainsi qu'il est requis" a mother
is instructing her daughter on the eve of the daughter's marriage to a known sodomist. The mother, a
practitioner of modesty, cannot name the *quid* and
the *quo.* Within the tantalizing discourse of modesty,
the *quid* and the *quo* are referred to in the context of
the whirling *quid pro quo:* "Since decency keeps me
from entering into certain details, I have but one
thing to advise you, my daughter, do not trust the
first propositions your husband makes you, and tell
him firmly: No, sir, it is not there that an honest
woman is taken, *everywhere else as much as you
please, but as for that, certainly not*" (14:117).

The mother prescribes resistance, not to any
specified act, but to "the first propositions your husband makes you," thus choreographing a movement
in which the first aggression is followed, on cue, by
resistance. The husband, with true perversity, turns
everything around: "out of a principle of modesty
and honesty . . . the prince, wanting to do things
according to the rules, at least for the first time, offers
his wife simply the chaste pleasures of wedlock"
(ibid.). The husband in his "modesty" falls into step

with the mother. The girl responds on cue: "For whom do you take me, sir, she tells him, did you imagine that I would consent to such things? *everywhere else as much as you please, but as for that, certainly not.*" So the young bride, tergiversating out of modesty, thinks she is turning her back upon her husband, when she is actually offering him her behind.

The husband has modesty to thank for this fortuitous switch: "and then fools took for a virtue what was simply an artificial refinement of libertinage." The same gesture, the same words can be interpreted as virtue or libertine spice depending upon whether the interpreter is a libertine or a fool. Although the two tellings of the story are otherwise in completely different words, the lines taught the girl by her mother and faithfully repeated remain the same: "*everywhere else as much as you please, but as for that, certainly not.*" Appearing thus four times in the two versions of the story, always in italics, the hauntingly repeated phrase becomes a point of opening onto the outside of the symmetrically framed story. The insistence of those same italicized words erodes the simple irony of the compact story. "Everywhere else" points, not to the other alternative in a binary opposition, but to a multiplicity of detours. "Tergiversation," *Le Petit Robert* informs us, is "almost always found in the plural."

The mother in "L'Epoux complaisant" unwittingly offers the same advice as Mme de Saint-Ange gives Eugénie: "Let her *indiscriminately offer in its place* her hand, her mouth, her tits, or her asshole" (my italics). The young bride ends up telling her husband that he can take his pleasure anywhere but in the vagina. Yet even were the simple ironic switch

not to have happened—had the husband made his
first move towards the anus (as the mother expected)—the bride would still have uttered those
equivocal words. Following her mother's instruc-
tions to the letter, she would have, in that case, en-
joined her husband to take his pleasure anywhere
but in the anus, still leaving him with the choice of a
multitude of perversions: "everywhere else as much
as you please." Those eerie words (always exactly
the same, their meaning totally dependent upon context) persist in a manner derisive of the either-or
situation the story appears to frame them in. The
story would appear merely subversive—turning a situation upside-down, laying a fine upstanding girl
bottomside-up. The insistent refrain opens onto a
truly perverse situation, spinning things all the way
around ("everywhere else") in an evocation of cen-
trifugal force. Tergiversation is not a simple one-step,
one-way substitution. Perversion (per-vertere, turn
completely around) sets up a radical quid pro quo in
which the quid and the quo have always been spinning around each other and any definition of one as
more original is itself part of the gay dance.

Once any exchange is possible, once the telos
(the vagina) is equated or equatable, then the substitutions can proliferate. The absolute value of a telos
means its value is not a function of anything, not
subordinate to any function. The possibility of an
equivalent relativizes the value. The very positing of
a substitute for the vagina assumes a grammar explaining that equivalency. That grammar opens the
door for a potentially unending series of paradigmatic equivalents. Although Mme de Saint-Ange
only names four ("her hand, her mouth, her tits, her
asshole"), a page later Dolmancé (Eugénie's other

teacher) adds the thighs and the armpits to the list. The list is limited only by the imaginative capacities of the compiler.

Tergiversation is a radically furtive business. From a simple "turn one's back," the substitution of back for front, the action slips to a proliferating whirl evidenced by the fact that "tergiversation" is "almost always found in the plural." It is this slippage that keeps the opposition anus / vagina from solidifying into a good / evil, true / false dichotomy, into two halves together accounting for the whole universe.

Nonetheless, sodomy "proper," because of its position at the entry to this slide, is for the post-1954 Klossowski the "key sign" in Sade's work of all the perversions. Sodomy is the key to the domain of integral atheism. "Integral" surprisingly appears in "Le Philosophe scélérat" on the side of all that which should pose the greatest threat to wholeness or integrity. Integral atheism is not the upright integrity of a principle to which one is faithful. Rather, it implies an equivocal "going all the way": a thorough compromise of reputation. She who goes all the way has not a vestige of propriety left to cling to. This use of "integral" is in keeping with the paradoxical aim Klossowski discovers in Sade's quest for excessive monstrosity: "*constancy* in inconsistency" (*SMP*67, p. 44). To be lacking in integrity through and through, one must be integrally monstrous. Klossowski explains that rationalistic, moral atheism "is still nothing other than an inverted monotheism" (*SMP*67, p. 20). Inversion (*invertere*, turn inside-out) is a univocal substitution which, while switching what is in and what is out, maintains the distinction inside and outside. As Klossowski explains, "By the same right as the notion of God, [this timid atheism] guarantees the responsible ego, its propriety, individual identity" (pp. 20–21). Integral atheism is unsatisfied with the simple substitution of the rational ego in God's place. It aims for a "universal prostitution of beings," a vertiginous spin erosive of individual identity, a perpetual masked ball. "Integral atheism signifies that the very principle of identity disappears with the absolute guarantor of this principle" (SMP67, p. 25).

Sodomy lends itself to the same distinction between cautious sodomy and integral sodomy. Sodomy seems to imply a simple substitution, as a result of which the couple male / female is replaced by the opposition active / passive. Yet through the strange logic of the *quid pro quo* this simple switch relentlessly slides into a more radical trifling with identities. The substitution anus for vagina not only makes possible but necessarily slips into the substitution boy for girl. After Mme de Saint-Ange strongly recommends to Eugénie the replacement of vaginal intercourse by anal intercourse, she asks Dolmancé to support her argument by a depiction of the joys of sodomy. Although he is supposed to be instructing a *girl,* Dolmancé cannot but say, "When one does so much just to be a bugger, Eugénie, one must be one completely. Fucking women in the ass is only being one halfway: it is in man that nature wants man to serve this caprice" (3:414).

With the replacement of the girl by a boy, active / passive becomes a reversible structure: "It's in man that nature wants man. . . ." The result of this reversibility is *not* egalitarian disappearance of roles. The link between active / passive and male / female is not erased; it is radicalized. If the male / female confrontation in "normal" coitus consists in the violent penetration of the passive, vulnerable vagina by the awesome, thrusting virile tool, then sodomy is more fucking than fucking. In sodomy the orifice is smaller and more delicate (more feminine), the penetration more violent and painful, the erect penis more awesome because of a greater discrepancy between it and the orifice. Buggering is a more successful representation of the fantasies surrounding the confrontation between the sexes (as separate sexes, marked by the emblems of sexual differentiation) than "normal" coitus.

Rather than provoking utopian, neo-moralistic talk about the transcendence of sexual differentiation through sodomy, the Sadian text poses the question of which is more transgressive, which more zestily criminal: violation of a male or female. On the eighteenth of the *120 Journées de Sodome*, the bishop interrupts Duclos's narration in order to voice his agreement with the hero of the passion being described, a man who goes to Duclos's brothel and asks for a young man in drag rather than a woman. The bishop agrees that a male is a better object for passion than a female. The president, Curval, disagrees. A discussion ensues which is not resolved.

The friends are disputing which side of the male / female duality would most satisfactorily fill the passive role in the active / passive opposition that sodomy has allowed to replace the male / female structure. However, in Duclos's story the young man requested is a "*masculine fouetteuse*" (masculine female flogger): that is, the boy for girl substitution occurs on the active side of the active / passive split. Any solid bi-univocal correspondence $\left(\frac{male}{female} \begin{smallmatrix} \bullet \\ \bullet \end{smallmatrix} \frac{active}{passive} \right)$ has been set completely aspin. Identity has be-

come a choreographed play of masks governed now
by the distinction client / whore.

The disparity between the bishop's advocacy of
the male over the female for the passive role and its
inspiration in a choice of male over female for the
active role reproduces the dizzying implications of
prostitution. Prostitution makes any clear notion of
which party is dominating an encounter impossible.
The whore (woman-as-truly-woman, ultimate femininity) is pure receptacle. Her form, mask, identity,
is not the expression of some inner essence, but a
response to the other's wishes. Her identity is the
other's. As amorphous receptacle,[8] capable of taking
any filling whatsoever, this extreme of femininity
that is the whore is even capable of containing
masculinity.

The couple client / whore is the ultimate form of
the opposition man / woman. According to a formu-
lation of Zarathustra: "Das Glück des Mannes heisst:
ich will. Das Glück des Weibes heisst: er will"
("Man's happiness means: I want. Woman's happiness means: he wants".)[9] The client's role is to demand his "I want." The whore plays out the "he
wants." In the renunciation of mastery (of the "ich
will") the woman encompasses and surpasses the
man; she knows what he wants.

This absolute degradation of identity is to be
distinguished from the timid whore, who separates
those roles she must play to earn a living from her
"real" life, her real "self." The wilder, integral whore
is an abyss of nonidentity, perpetually masked by
well-determined roles imprinted through contact
with the other's desire. The john rules the whore,
leads the dance, gets his way. Yet the whore can also
play the ruler, if that is desired; thus she is the deri-

.

sion of the opposition ruler / ruled. The whore can be the client if the client would choose to be the whore.

The whore, as feminine, stealthy erosion of masculine responsibility, selfsameness, and uprightness, is another name for the passive role in sodomy. The *120 Journées* question of the superiority of male or female, asked once in the context of the active role (the *masculine fouetteuse*), repeated in the context of the passive role (victims of the libertines' violations), becomes the question of which is preferable: active or passive role. "It has often been questioned which of these two ways [active and passive] of committing sodomy is the most voluptuous: it is undoubtedly the passive . . . ; it is so sweet to change sexes, so delicious to counterfeit a whore" (*Philosophie*, 3:431).

The speaker is Dolmancé, who earlier has said, "One must be completely [a bugger]. Fucking women in the ass is only being one halfway." The switch from vagina to anus must be completed by the switch from girl to boy. However, that double substitution still leaves a stationary point of reference, a subject responsible for the choice of receptacles for the penis, unique emblem of a unified subject. The imperative to be completely a bugger is unremitting in its perversity. The true buggerer must become the buggeree. The play of substitutions infects the substituting agent. The stationary point is caught up in the dance, changing sex, putting on the mask of the harlot. If the whore is the wearer of masks *par excellence*, whose only attribute is a perpetual counterfeit, then the only proper (which is to say, improper) manner to be a whore is "to counterfeit a whore." The whore is not true to herself. The sodomized man, as counterfeit whore, is in his very falsity a true whore.

Dolmancé, settling down from his lyrical effusion in praise of being buggered, regains cognizance of the fact that his discourse is supposed to be subordinate to his role as Eugénie's teacher. Is not the buggeree's sweetness ("to change sexes") limited to men? "But Eugénie," Dolmancé continues, "let us stick to some advice on details, relating only to those women who, metamorphosed into men, wish to enjoy this delicious pleasure" (3:431). Through the bizarre logic of the *quid pro quo*, integral sodomy brings about not only the metamorphosis of man into woman, but also of woman into man. "This delicious pleasure" ("it is so delicious to counterfeit a whore") institutes a wild trifling with identity in which the woman whose anus is penetrated plays a man playing a whore / woman. If the man is a false (that is to say, true) whore, then the woman as false man is a false counterfeit (in other words, an authentic) whore. The authentic whore is false in her very falseness. She need not be true to her "self" (i.e., false). The question, then, of which is the truer whore (the truer essentially false creature) is gaily undecidable.

According to Klossowski, integral sodomy as the radical violation of the propriety of either sex finds its complementary image in the Androgyne. This point of fascination for post-1954 Klossowski's Sade—the androgyne—is inscribed in a chain of substitutions, inheriting a tradition from the other side of the 1950s break in Klossowski's *oeuvre*. Klossowski's encounter with Sade produces three successive female figures (Klossowski specifies that "Sade elaborates . . . the simulacrum of the Androgyne: not as a man-woman, but as a woman-man" [*SMP*67, p. 48]), marking the three disjointed stages of that confrontation.

In 1933 Klossowski publishes his first work on Sade, a rather traditional psychoanalytic piece concentrating on the image of the mother, where he elaborates upon Sade's negative Oedipus complex and the primary importance of the maternal figure as type of the Sadian victim.[10] However, the apotheosis of this maternal victim is Justine, who in her maidenhood underlines the dangers besetting any attempt to apply a too-literal, too-reductive Freudian schema to literature, a schema which makes the maternal role so literal that it cannot be comfortably played by a maiden.

By the first edition of *Sade mon prochain* the mother figure has been overlaid by the central image of the virgin, a substitution prefigured by Justine's importance in the earlier work. The switch of focus from mother to virgin bears witness to a change in perspective from psychoanalytic to Christian. Excerpts from the earlier article are included as an appendix to the 1947 book: "for documentary reasons, I am reproducing here a few excerpts from my article" (*SMP*67, p. 189, n.). The appendix serves more than an impartial historical function ("for documentary reasons") for Klossowski, who will later be so concerned with the relation, or lack of it, between his texts from different periods.[11] Klossowski, in the first edition of *Sade mon prochain*, is *already* trying to appropriate and tame an earlier divergent stage of his work. This gesture becomes explicit in the 1967 reedition of the book, which is heralded as "a double reading: while confronting *Sade mon prochain* with

'Sade ou le philosophe scélérat' . . . . Pierre Klossowski conducts a second stage of his meditation
about Sade" (back cover of SMP67). However this
"second stage" follows a first stage that is already not
original, that tries to dissimulate its divergence from
an even earlier period.

In the 1947 appendix, Klossowski does not
merely reproduce portions of the old article; he re-
works it, trying to explain the transference from
mother to virgin through a developmental view of
psychology. In the beginning, the child believes in
the mother's purity: the mother and the virgin are
thus originally synonymous. Through some contingency, suspicion enters the child's head, making him
aware of the mother's carnality, guilt, impurity. At
that moment the "adorable element" separates off
from the mother and attaches itself to the virgin
proper. Klossowski begins this proof of the essential
identity of the Freudian discussion of the mother and
the Christian elaboration of the virgin with a prolep-
tic acknowledgment of the appearance of conflict
between those two moments of his encounter with
Sade: "At first glance, these reflections seem to contradict those I developed thirteen years later in the
chapter on Homage to the Virgin [chapter of 'Sous le
masque de l'athéisme']. However the secret motif of
hatred of the Mother . . . could be closer to the resentment directed at the virgin than one might admit" (SMP47, p. 198).

By the time of the 1967 reedition, the difference
between 1933 and 1947 has become unworthy of
mention. The appendix in question is included in
the reedition with a single change. The first sentence
in the above quotation is extracted, taking along with
it the "however" of the second sentence. In the 1947

edition this passage is preceded by a break in the text, dividing the appendix into two parts and consequently emphasizing this, the beginning of the second part. In 1967 there is no break and the paragraph explaining the transference from Mother to Virgin quietly begins: "The secret motif of hatred of the Mother . . . could be closer to the resentment directed at the virgin than one might admit" (*SMP67*, p. 184). The tranquillity of the affirmation, made possible by an unmentioned erasure (in this 1967 book that is supposedly explicit about its divergences from the 1947 edition) of marks of the conflict between 1933 and 1947, is broken only by the now slightly odd "closer . . . than one might admit"—a remark most comprehensible as a reference to the sentence removed.

The virgin, retroactively instated as unchallenged primary female figure of *Sade mon prochain* 1947, can then be posited as forerunner to 1967's androgyne. In the introduction to the reedition Klossowski criticizes himself-as-author-of-the-1947-book for not having seen that the image of the virgin "inasmuch as she signifies the *death of the instinct of procreation*" is simply "a (monotheistic) normalization of the myth of the *Androgyne*" (*SMP67*, p. 14). In other words, the virgin is able to be a predecessor to the androgyne inasmuch as the former means the death of maternity. By the time of the androgyne (*SMP67*), the traces of the mother's threat to the virgin ("these reflections seem to contradict") have been, for the most part, erased. Although originally synonymous with the mother, the virgin now "signifies the *death of the instinct of procreation*." Juliette, representative of the androgyne, figures in the early, psychoanalytic article on the mother as

"the 'tribade' (that is the woman without social obligation) as opposed to the social ideal of the mother"
(*SMP*67, p. 182). Thus the androgyne not only is an
ideal transcendence of the distinction male / female,
but also traces its roots to both sides of the 1933
opposition mother / lesbian.

Klossowski, in 1967, condemns the virgin image
of 1947 for "a romanticism in which the author con-
fesses to have delighted not long ago, but for which
he must today reject his *pious intention*" (*SMP*67, p.
14). Yet as ideal resolution to the undecidable and
unending argument over which is better, male or
female, the androgyne betrays a sizable investment
of romantic idealism. The exuberant coda of the 1963
preface to *Aline et Valcour* (Klossowski's first mention of the Sadian androgyne and first post-1950 text
on Sade) refers to "the androgyne, the ideal most
desperately coveted by Sade."[12]

"Androgyne" (man-woman) is defined by *Le Petit Robert* (p. 60) as "*an individual of the masculine
sex in whom the lower segment of the genital appa-
ratus has evolved according to the feminine type*"
(my italics). Yet Klossowski scrupulously specifies
(*SMP*67, p. 48) that Sade's androgyne is not a "man-
woman" (andro-gyne), but a "woman-man" (gyne-an-
dro), an individual of the feminine sex having virile
characteristics. Juliette usurps the title androgyne
through a dizzying double violation of sexual limi
tations by which gynandry becomes androgyny. Juliette's status as androgyne, rather than being a frank
resolution of the unbearable either-or tension,
achieves its full transgressive potency as a subversion made possible by the rules of the game of sexual
difference. Juliette is not a true androgyne, but the

whore-as-androgyne, counterfeit ideal as response to the "desperate covetousness."

The effect of carefully registering the androgyne on the feminine side of the roster (the side of whorish falsity) is a degradation of the male-identified notion of androgyny by which it loses its selfsameness and integrity. What begins in 1963 as "the ideal most desperately coveted by Sade" becomes in 1967 "the simulacrum of the androgyne" (*SMP67*, p. 48). "Gyn-andry" (the transcendence of difference "rightfully" belonging on the female side) is defined as "the condition *of a female* in which the external genitalia *simulate* those of a male"[13] (my italics). The female manner of transgression of sexual identity is simulation: the production of simulacra.

1963: Klossowski puts forth the androgyne and the simulacrum; however, they have not yet realized their common destiny as "the simulacrum of the androgyne." In this year in which he introduces the androgyne into his encounter with Sade, Klossowski writes once again on his friend Georges Bataille (the first time since 1950), publishing "A propos du simulacre dans la communication de Georges Bataille." Whereas his two earlier pieces on Bataille ("Le Corps du néant" and "La Messe de Georges Bataille") contain explicit references to Sade, in this homage to Bataille the marquis's name does not appear. But the entire article is informed by the structures which are at play in the post-1950 Klossowski reading of Sade. Bataille's "atheology" repeats Sade's "integral atheism" (when both are written by Klossowski's pen):

Whoever says *atheology* is concerned with the *divine vacancy*, that is, with the place specifically held by the *name of God*—God guarantor of the personal ego. Whoever says *atheology* also says *vacancy of the ego*.[14]

Integral atheism signifies that the very principle of identity disappears with the absolute guarantor of that principle; thus that the propriety of the responsible ego is
morally and physically abolished.

In this 1963 text on Bataille, Klossowski asserts
that Bataille does not speak in concepts, but in simulacra of concepts, for his aim is not intelligible
communication, but complicity. Bataille is thus like
a Sadian character: "It is not by arguments that the
Sadian character can get the interlocutor's adhesion
but by complicity" (SMP67, p. 35). Sadian libertines
form secret societies based on complicity, and in
these nests of accomplices, sodomy becomes a simulacrum, not a meaningful act but a rite of complicity.

Sadian sodomy is a rite worthy of the Nietzschean Church of the Death of God—locus of Klossowski's tergiversations about Bataille in "Le Corps
du néant." According to Klossowski, among "the
amorphous mass of those that we [the Christian
friends] consider unbelievers" there are those who
try to form "across from the Church, counter-
churches where counter-theologies are preached"
(SMP47, p. 155). These counter-churches (plural as
opposed to the uniqueness of the one true Church)
are the ecclesiastical analogue of the bodily orifices
(frequently referred to by Sadian characters as "al-
tars") other than the vagina. The vagina as seat of
procreation of the species is the organ of generality.
Sodomy, entrance to the slide leading off into the
plurality of tergiversations, focuses on the anus,
which is situated *across from the vagina.* "Across
from Golgotha they raise anti-Golgothas at whose
feet they celebrate an eternal Holy Friday against any
paschal apprehension" (p. 155). At Golgotha God
dies on Holy Friday, but that death is teleologically

subordinate to the Resurrection and salvation for the human race. Penile-vaginal intercourse is expenditure of energy in the service of the human race, death for the sake of birth. Anal intercourse spends energy uselessly ("a Holy Friday against any paschal apprehension").

"Having 'killed God' within himself, Nietzsche at the same time destroyed the world where a communicability of experiences is possible" (*SMP*47, p. 176). The death of God is the advent of the simulacrum. The anus cannot propagate the human race, cannot further community, communication, and communion between individuals; it only produces waste matter. Klossowski's Bataille, member of the Church of the Death of God, "justly negates communication, because one could never communicate anything but the remains [*déchet*, waste material] of what one claims to communicate. . . . The simulacrum is all we know of an experience: the notion is only its remains [*déchet*] summoning other remains [*déchets*]" ("A propos du simulacre," p. 743).

Klossowski, the Christian of "Le Corps du néant," would reappropriate the church of his "unbelieving friends" into the true Church. The true Church encompasses the Church of the Death of God, includes God's death on Holy Friday. A counter-church (and "every counter-Church is the Church of the Death of God," (*SMP*47, p. 180) is a body without a head, without Christ. Christ, the head, is the condition of possibility for communication between the members of the body, the Church. Klossowski's Nietzsche could not communicate his experience of the Death of God to his disciples (the members of the Nietzschean Church of the Death of God) because that experience itself negates any communication:

"effectively, God alone allows men to understand each other and, if God dies, they no longer understand each other" (*SMP*47, p. 182). Klossowski's reincorporation of the Church of the Death of God into the Church of the Resurrection makes possible the communication of the experience of that Death.

Klossowski closes the 1948 article "De l'opportunité à étudier l'oeuvre du marquis de Sade" with a plug for the application of Christian exegesis to profane writing "and most particularly [to the writings] which were written against [*contre*, counter to] the Holy Scriptures" (p. 721). Christianity can comprehend that which is written against it. New horizons of the human heart can be opened up "thanks to the very key to the Scriptures: Jesus Christ who, by renouncing his divinity for an ignominious death, subjected to his Spirit the worlds which contest the Spirit." Jesus Christ is the possibility of communication, the key to comprehension of any writing, not through his divinity, or even his paradoxical humano-divinity, but through his "ignominious death."

Ignominy is the loss of name *(in-nomen*, without name). Absolute loss of name is not simply loss of one's good name, of one's reputation, but total loss of identity, leading to integral prostitution, to lack of selfsameness. Through this debasing loss of honor, reputation, and self, Christ "subjected to his Spirit the worlds which contest the Spirit." Christ dominates his opponents, not through a frank, virile show of God's force, but through the underhanded, feminine ploys of the whore. He undermines his opposition by tampering with identity—the necessary foundation of a solid polarity. The counter-church is encompassed by the true Church; the worlds contesting the Spirit are under the domination of the Spirit.

Christ triumphs, rusefully, in Klossowski's pre-1950s writing.

Post-1950s, in the reedition of *Sade mon prochain*, "Le Corps du néant" has silently disappeared—*supprimée* in the reedition of 1967," as the *Arc* bibliography puts it—and "Le Philosophe scélérat" noisily appears. "Placed at the head of the reedition of the old work, ["Le Philosophe scélérat"] is not only supposed to mark everything which opposes the author to his first conception, but besides, if possible, it is supposed to fill a grave lacuna" (*SMP*67, p. 11). The lacuna to be filled is not the place of the missing "Corps du néant," but the incompletion of "L'Esquisse du système." However the head ("placed at the head") of the 1967 book inherits an unexpected legacy from the *supprimé* (suppressed, omitted, abolished, killed, liquidated, done away with) headless body ("Le Corps du néant" refers to the acephalic Nietzschean Church). Christ ("the very key to the Scriptures") is replaced by sodomy ("the key sign to all the perversions"). In the Christian Church,

the communication of experience flows from the communication between the head of the mystical Body [Christ] and its members. [*SMP*47, p. 183]

Starting from [the sodomite act] . . . Sade projects perversion into the domain of thought, where integral monstrosity forms something like a space of spirits communicating between themselves through the mutual intelligence of this key sign. [*SMP*67, p. 37]

This subversion linking Christ, the head of the true Church, to sodomy, a rite of the headless counter-church, is not a simple inversion by which a term passes from one side of a static opposition to another. Christ of the Ignominious Death, Christ the nonidentical floozie, can encompass her opposite (the counter-church, "the writings against [contre] the Holy Scriptures," "the worlds that contest the Spirit"). Sodomy as simulacrum operates a wild falsification, not only counterfeiting everything but making everything counterfeit. Sodomy "is pronounced by a specific gesture of contre-généralité" (SMP67, p. 32). Yet just as in 1947 Klossowski's Christ pulls off an appropriation of the counter-church proving the counter-church to be already included in the Christian church; so in 1967 the counter-generality is "already implicit in the existing generality" (SMP67, p. 34). Brazen perversity (as in the effect of the haunting refrain of "L'Epoux complaisant") is not found in the upside-down switch ("inverted monotheism") but in a thorough disruption of identity through which the possibility of a counter-order has already contaminated the "original" order. The farthest-flung, most "integral" atheism can only attain to a prostitution already the (stolen) property of Christ of the Ignominious Death.

Sodomy in "Le Philosophe scélérat" thus not only violates selfsame sexual identity through its contagious counterfeiting, but it institutes a freeflowing exchange between individuals unimpeded by the rigid borders imposed by such identities. Anal intercourse is the keystone of a system enabling the individual pervert, locked into his singularity, to engage in a generalized exchange. This system "born of the Death of God" (SMP47, p. 169) establishes, not a general reciprocity of persuasion (the aim of notions and concepts), but a counter-generality of complicity. Here where penis meets anus is the zone where individual perverts transcend their absolutely specific perversions and mingle with others with whom they have nothing in common except a position outside the normative generality of the human race. Sodom, of the title *120 Journées de Sodome,* is the meeting-place where all the perversions collect. The counter-generality of complicity, the affinity of all these perverts, is founded upon the fluidity of sodomy as simulacrum. Anal intercourse's constant propensity to slide off into a multiplicity of other acts—its lack of honorable selfsameness—evidences the fact that this act not only violates the identity of its perpetrators, but has itself an eroded identity.

In English the definition of "sodomy" reflects its self-transgressing nature. In one dictionary "sodomy" is defined as "1. Anal copulation of one male with another. 2. In some legal usage, anal or oral copulation with a member of the opposite sex or any copulation with an animal."[15] In another dictionary "sodomy" has lost its central, specific meaning— "anal copulation of one male with another" (the only meaning listed for *sodomie* in *Le Petit Robert*)—having come to mean the counter-generality as a whole (and not "a specific gesture of *contre-généralité*"), and thus is only defined generically: "carnal copulation with a member of the same sex or with an animal; noncoital carnal copulation with a member of the opposite sex."[16] Sodomy slips from a single scrupulously specific act (a true perversion) to everything but a single specific act (all carnal copulation except penile-vaginal coitus). "For Sade, the sodomite act . . . should . . . constitute the principle of affinity between the perversions" (*SMP* 67, p. 37). The simulacrum sodomy in its lack of self-possessed identity brings the perversions together. Sodom as the meeting-place of perverts provides the setting for an ami able conjunction, not structured by the meticulous rules of the specific perversions: "the affinity of one pervert for another permits a mutual overstepping of their particular cases" (SMP67, p. 26).

Dolmancé, in the company of those he continually refers to as "my friends," proves unfaithful to his own perversion. In the course of his instruction, he penetrates Eugénie's vagina with his tongue, through his own initiative. "This pretty little virgin cunt deliciously offers itself to me. I am a culprit, a criminal, I know; such charms are hardly made for my eyes; but the desire to give this child the first lessons in *volupté* outweighs any other consideration" (*Philosophie*, 3:426). In the relaxed atmosphere of Mme de Saint-Ange's boudoir, Dolmancé transgresses his own identity as bugger. This sodomite has begun to tumble down the slide from sodomy in its primary sense ("anal copulation of one male with another," Dolmancé's "to be completely a bugger") to sodomy as the entire realm of the counter-generality (which includes "oral copulation with a member of the opposite sex").

His affinity with his companions echoed by the affinity of all the acts of the counter-generality (loose definition of "sodomy") leads Dolmancé to wish to prostitute himself to his friends' desires. It is Mme de Saint-Ange's wish that he instruct her protégée. Yet Saint-Ange's wish has kindled Dolmancé's desire: "such charms are hardly made for my eyes" is contradicted by "this pretty little virgin cunt which deliciously offers itself to me." Dolmancé becomes a "criminal" through two desires. The first is "the desire to give this child the first lessons in *volupté*." This is originally Mme de Saint-Ange's idea, thus Saint-Ange plays the client to Dolmancé's whore.

Just as Juliette, the hussy, announces, "I am only really inflamed by their desires [the desires of others, of men]" (*Juliette*, 9:86); so Dolmancé's ardor in response to Saint-Ange's lesson plan is reflected in the correspondence between the "*desire to give* . . . the *first* lessons" and the "*virgin* cunt which *deliciously* offers itself" (my italics in both phrases). Dolmancé goes on: "I want to make her 'come' flow . . . I want to exhaust her, if possible . . . (He tongues her.)" Dolmancé's second desire is to make Eugénie show proof of her desire. Eugénie becomes the client. Dolmancé is aroused by the anticipated arousal of Eugénie. The whore's goal is the client's satisfaction.

Mme de Saint-Ange's brother, the Chevalier, also is to be found prostituting himself (being unfaithful to his own desires) to his friends, in the name of friendship. "As a matter of fact," he explains to his sister, "I like women, myself, and I only indulge in these bizarre tastes when an amiable man urges. There is nothing I wouldn't do in that case" (3:373). The Chevalier tells his sister of a previous meeting with Dolmancé, at which the latter expresses his wish to be fucked by the Chevalier. Saint-Ange's brother, although playing the active role, the male role, assumes the role of the whore in this situation, acting, as he does, solely out of compliance with Dolmancé's wishes. He describes the course of the copulation to Saint-Ange: "I treated Dolmancé like a friend; the excessive pleasure he was tasting, his wrigglings, his delicious words, everything soon made me happy myself, and I inundated him" (3:374). He begins "like a friend"—without any wish of his own, without any arousal of his own for this act—he ends, a true floozie, like Juliette, excited in response to the other's desire.

The Chevalier's whoring affords Dolmancé the opportunity to "counterfeit a whore"—the consequence, for a man, of being buggered. The scene: one whore in the ass of another, a scene made possible because the Chevalier treated Dolmancé "like a friend." Friendship provides an opening onto possibilities not merely for a thorough theatricalisation of the active / passive structure (making it counterfeit, making it profoundly nonserious), but for a disruption of the solidity of the client / whore relation whereby not only does the whore play a client, but her? his? lack of integrity and selfsameness ineradicably besmirches the client's name, his? her? very identity.

Like Noirceuil, who "only controverted so as better to make his friends shine," the Chevalier fucks Dolmancé as a friend in a comfortable, gay situation typical of Sade's work. The extravagant orgies structuring the action in the Sadian text celebrate the conjuncture of friends: friends prostituting themselves to each other, for each other. "There is nothing as delicious as for several friends of similar taste and similar spirit to be able to get together thusly; they communicate their ideas, their proclivities to each other; the desires of some are lit by the irregularities of the others' desire; they outdo, surpass, encourage each other, and the results are divine" (*Nouvelle Justine*, 7:165–66). These gatherings provide the perfect situation for any floozie who like Juliette is only excited in response to the other's desires. What Klossowski designates as "the ascesis of apathy," the limit-point of "integral monstrosity," the possibility for the pervert to transcend his enslavement to his own desires in an apathetic, constant reiteration of transgressive acts, occurs through monstrous characters' momentary amical relations with each other ("the affinity of one pervert for another permits a mutual overstepping of their particular cases"). The eminently sociable meetings of the outrageous libertines, in whorishly inconstant and whorishly compliant friendship, are the locus of any such possible ascesis.

The instructive cavorting of friends in *La Philosophie dans le boudoir* builds to the climax of Eugénie getting her wish to torment her mother. Yet by the end of the seven dialogues constituting the integral violation of Eugénie, "the universal prostitution of beings" has made a mockery of the designation "her wish." Through a typically Sadian gesture of unmasking the counter-generality (prostitution of identity) implicit in the generality (the normative institutions of society), Eugénie plays the role of pupil to the hilt. Her prostitution is not the result of a perversion of the pupil role, but a reflection of the violation to integrity characteristic of that role played straight. Mme de Saint-Ange, the schoolmistress, explains the dynamics of education: "We inflame her with our fires, we will feed her with our philosophy, we will instill in her our desires" (3:375).

Eugénie the pupil, like Juliette the slut, stands ready to bear the imprint of the other. Empty of any wish or idea of her own, she becomes aroused by the contact with the other's desire or thought. Counterfeit: *contra-facere*, make-against, make by the application of pressure (by something placed) against the object-to-be. The authenticity of a coin is founded upon its fidelity to the paradigmatic form of that coin. The most authentic coin is the best copy, the truest counterfeit.

Eugénie's lack of integrity, her role as amorphous matter always ready to be formed, is belied by her constant wish to kill her mother. At the end of the book, Eugénie's wish appears about to be fulfilled; her mother is in her hands. However, the mother is not killed, and the torture has been expropriated, become not-Eugénie's, to such a degree that the girl never notices that her wish has been distorted, perverted, *contrefait* (the French adjective meaning "counterfeit" also means "deformed"). The torture of Mme de Mistival is directed by Dolmancé, who, speaking in a tone described as "coldblooded," prefaces his decree of Eugénie's mother's fate with, "Well now, my friends, in my capacity as your teacher" (3:545). Perpetrating his crime "cold-bloodedly," realizing Klossowski's "ascesis of apathy," is made possible by his role of instructor. Here in this revelry among friends ("Well now, my friends") the teacher is no less a slut than his pupil. Dolmancé teaches in response to Saint-Ange's project to educate Eugénie. Dolmancé takes over Eugénie's wish to torment her mother: the pupil-as-whore plays the john to the teacher-as-whore's whore.

Not only does he direct Eugénie's desire, but in true counterfeit style Dolmancé becomes hot and bothered by the contact with her ardor and appropriates her incestuous consummation (her only act based upon her own wishes in the book). The original plan, formed by Dolmancé and Saint-Ange, is that, after the mother has been violated fore and aft by a syphilitic servant of Dolmancé, "Eugénie must . . . carefully sew up both cunt and ass" (3:546). Watching the daughter sew up her mother's cunt, Dolmancé is aroused to the point where he can no longer contain himself: "Eugénie, yield the ass to me,

it's my part" (3:547). Dolmancé in his role as partisan
of asses can, in a perverse way, lay claim to any ass.
Even on the body of another, they are his part of the
body: "what [the pervert] feels most is the other's
body as being his," (*SMP* 67, p. 47). He grabs the
needle from his pupil and ecstatically carries out the
plan in Eugénie's place, even to the point of calling
Mme de Mistival "darling mama" (ibid.). The end (of
the act) belongs to Dolmancé. Eugénie's integral
prostitution is accomplished as her teacher usurps
her original identity, her own "origin," steals her
very mother.

The introduction to the 1967 edition of *Sade
mon prochain* declares that "Le Philosophe scélérat"
continues the unfinished progression of the early
work "Esquisse du système de Sade." Yet the version
of that study found in the 1967 book—a text that
certainly conforms with and points to the lead article
of the reedition—is substantially different from the
"Esquisse du système" found in the 1947 edition.
Except for its first paragraphs, the fifth and final
section of the "Esquisse" has been entirely rewritten.
Klossowski's systematic attempt to read Sade's opus
as a dialectical progression culminates—in 1947 (and
in 1934 when the piece was first published)—in a
moral of aggressivity linked to a traditional psychoanalytic view of primary egocentrism. This 1947
"ascesis of apathy," the limit-point of Klossowski's
Sadian system, is the accomplishment of a negation
of other people and an exaltation of the ego "taken to
its limit." In 1967, the fifth chapter of the "Esquisse,"
with its "ascesis of apathy," celebrates the abolition
of the ego along with other people, in a universal

prostitution of beings. The culmination of the system in 1967 has been placed out of the realm of possibilities for the individual-as-unified-individual (true to himself), being possible only as the feat of a bunch of floozies.

The 1947 version of the "Esquisse" allows the complete transcendence of the notion of evil to be an aim for the individuated ego. The potential for reaching such a goal is based upon a return to a primordial state of the ego before it becomes civilized, before it is forced to recognize the other. Each individual is born with a dose of cruelty. That natural cruelty is distorted by the imposed contact with the world of other people where "normal," "healthy" aggressivity becomes unnatural evil. The renaturalization of cruelty demands a return to the state of primary egocentrism with a concomitant denial of the world of other people in favor of the *propre monde,* the world totally belonging to the individual ego, where the ego is absolute sovereign. The ego seeks to return to its original purity, to its original egocentric innocence. Thus the 1947 version of the "Esquisse" provides the lead-in to the study of destruction and purity centered on the figure of the virgin—innocence wholly intact, unviolated by the demands of the world of other people.

In 1967 Klossowski states that he erroneously was led from the "Esquisse" to the virgin, when he should have proceeded in the direction of the androgyne, the simulacrum, the whore: that is, in the direction of the "Philosophe scélérat." The changes in the 1967 edition of the "Esquisse" make such a claim possible. In the final version of that article the renaturalization of cruelty no longer leads to the purity and innocence of a primordial egocentrism. Other people and the world of others are no longer viewed as something secondary and external that comes to compromise the original ego's *propre monde.* The individuated ego too is a secondary elaboration. "The dose of cruelty with which nature has provided more or less each individual would thus be only the thwarted impulse of desire [that is, already secondary], with which each person identifies in primary egocentrism, as if it were one's tool, when this impulse would tend to destroy one as much as it tends to the destruction of others" (*SMP67*, pp. 131–32). Primary egocentrism is not originary, but is the result of an act of identification with the already perverted impulse of desire. The individuated ego is constituted through identification with an aggressive force apparently directed at other people, and actually just as dangerous to that ego. Thus other people are implicated in the ego's very constitution. The 1947-style attempt to purify the naturally cruel ego by negating the world of others is, in 1967, seen to concurrently negate the ego constituted as a relation to that world.

The 1967 ascesis of apathy, "in which the ego abolishes itself along with the other" (*SMP67*, p. 136), fits right in with the "Philosophe scélérat." In fact, a great number of the very sentences in the 1967 version of the fifth chapter of the "Esquisse" also appear in the section of the "Philosophe scélérat" entitled "L'ascèse de l'apathie." It is as if, in the firm belief that the 1947 version properly leads to the 1967 *Tel Quel* article and not to the romanticized discussion of the virgin, the rewriting[17] had been forgotten. Nonetheless, if the destruction of the ego really is inextricably implicated in the destruction of the other, then the 1967-style "ascesis of apathy" is already implicit in the 1947 version of the "Esquisse." "Esquisse" 1947 tends toward the Virgin; "Esquisse" 1967 points to the Androgyne. The possibility of 1967 lies dormant within 1947, just as the Androgyne is hidden behind the normalizing image of the Virgin.

The transfer from the constant integrity of the virgin to the simulacrum of the androgyne is, however, not a unidirectional correction (like Patri's Bataille for Sade) but a secret complicity between the virgin and the androgyne constituting an infidelity on the part of both in respect to their identities. Only from the vantage point of 1967, locus of the announcement of the universal prostitution of beings with its correlative erosion of ego-identity, can the affinity of the androgyne and the virgin be perceived. Virgin and androgyne alike (along with the mother that precedes them in this feminine parade) are the assumed names, the stolen identities, of a creature so unfaithful to any masculine notion of self or identity that the only proper name for her is the improper name "whore": not the proper title of any profession, even the scandalous "oldest profession," but the epithet hurled by others upon the one who has lost her reputation, lost her name, upon the one who has a bad name, a false name, always the wrong name.

Klossowski centers the Sadian virgin image upon Justine, the androgyne upon her sister Juliette. The exposure of the androgyne as the "true face" behind the virgin's mask unveils Juliette as the truth of Justine. Klossowski's substitution repeats Sade's replacement of Justine as narrator with Juliette as narrator.[18] Fraternization (sororization) between the two supposedly antinomous siblings is possible within the space of narration. In the first two versions of the novel, they meet when Justine tells her story to Juliette. In the final version they are together for Juliette to tell her tale to Justine.

The mutual contamination and the role switching can be set against the backdrop of *120 Journées,* in which the narrator's role belongs to the prostitute. The perversion of the notion of prostitution to a point where prostitution endangers the identity of the client makes the question of which is the greater whore—the constantly inconstant Juliette or the inconstantly constant Justine—indecidable in the manner of the question of the superior impropriety of the male or female buggeree. Just as the distinction male / female never dissolves (in fact, is absolutely necessary) in the vertiginous whirl of sodomistic counterfeiting, so the difference between Justine's and Juliette's modes of whoring is never erased. Nonetheless the two antinomous sisters (the virgin and the androgyne) meet and mingle in a lighter mood in that exuberant manifestation of virginal readiness—Eugénie de Mistival.

The reader of the Pauvert edition of the *Histoire de Juliette* encounters, in the prefatory pages to the story proper (pages not attributable to Sade), two comparisons between Juliette and another of Sade's female characters. The editors have inserted the now classic quotation from Apollinaire interpreting the duality Justine / Juliette that structures over four thousand pages of Sade's writing: "Justine is the old woman, subjugated, miserable and less than human; Juliette, on the contrary, represents the new woman he glimpses, a being we cannot conceive of, that breaks loose from humanity, that will have wings and will renew the universe."[19] Humanity is the community of men. Justine is subhuman: woman as less than man, the whore as man's servant. Juliette is superhuman: woman in her integral flightiness, light and heady, able to fly off and transcend man and his serious attempt at integrity and ego-identical domination, the floozie as that which surpasses man while falsifying his identity. Juliette represents "a being we cannot conceive of, that breaks loose from humanity": the whore in her radical feminity has the potential for the Nietzschean superman.

These liminal pages of the first volume of *Juliette* also include a preface by André Pieyre de Mandiargues in which the heroine of that novel is compared with the ingénue of *La Philosophie dans le boudoir*: "Eugénie de Mistival, who is to Juliette what a rose is to the one which will open a bit later on the same rosebush" (ibid., p. ii). The adolescent in her rite of passage is the mature rose; the full-blown heroine, some ten years Eugénie's senior, is the bud on the rosebush. Mandiargues agrees with Apollinaire that Juliette is an admirable creature, but for him Justine's sister does not mark the acme of Sade's female production. She merely promises future glory, represents "a being we cannot conceive of." Eugénie blossoms forth with the glory Juliette promises.

The correspondence of bud to woman-in-bloom and flower-in-bloom to budding adolescent maintains a certain tension through its inversion of the usual association. The perversity continues even after a return to the "normal" order that, following this inversion and the subsequent reversion, is no longer the same, for its absoluteness as the only possible order has been once and for all undermined: "As for love, it cannot be denied that Sade granted a certain share of it to Juliette, nevertheless less gener-

ously than to Eugénie de Mistival, who seems his
favorite as she is mine and about whom I already
said that she is the same heroine left in the delicious
state of a rough draft" (ibid., p. vi). The ingénue
Eugénie is here the rough draft; the full-grown
woman the final version. Yet the "normal" order has
been irreparably tampered with. The usual association implies a teleological subordination of the before to the after—the rough draft to the final copy.
Here, however, the heroine "left in the delicious state
of a rough draft" is favored, the incomplete accorded
the most love.

Apollinaire's Juliette represents the new superhuman woman escaping from the old female condition of servitude. Pieyre de Mandiargues's Eugénie
marks a further remove along that flight: setting off
an a-teleological insubordination, freeing the rough
draft from its subordinate position in reference to
male humanity's utilitarian principles. The insurrection is built upon the unfinished product's ability to
be delicious, to arouse in the perceiver a perverse
taste for its very incompletion. Eugénie incites Dolmancé to violate his principles of "proper" masculine identity through her "pretty little virgin cunt
that deliciously offers itself." The virgin cunt offers a
rough draft, an unfinished product (the cunt fulfills
its destiny as cunt only by being fucked), provoking
a complicitous urge to finish it. The rough draft has
not yet achieved its final identity, demands to be
formed. Eugénie as rough draft makes possible the
meeting of Juliette, the finished whore "who deliciously offers herself," and Justine, the "pretty little
virgin cunt."

Eugénie's book covers but a day of her life; the
sisters' stories last thirty years. Eugénie: a brilliant

moment of conjuncture between the too-reliably inconstant whore and the slight, provocative incon-
stancy of the constant virgin. Pieyre de Mandiargues
accentuates Eugénie's common filiation with Juliette:
both are initiated into the brotherhood of libertinage,
both take to their instruction with the enthusiastic
openness of a star pupil, shedding prejudice after
prejudice as the book proceeds, erasing the imprint
of a prior education in order to better receive the new
impression. On the other hand, despite Eugénie's
natural proclivities to wantonness and Justine's
nearly constant, frigid virtue, the young Mistival and
Juliette's sister also display a common heritage. Justine, constantly violated, maintains an ineradicable
virginal honor. Eugénie too has a magically reconstituting virtue: as each new man is introduced into the
dialogue Eugénie blushes and protests with virginal
modesty and indignation in seeming contradiction
with her eagerness for the various indecent acts in
which she has already indulged. At the moment of
the Chevalier's arrival, Eugénie has just had an or-
gasm while performing fellatio upon Dolmancé, after
having vied with Saint-Ange for "the honor of suck-
ing this handsome cock" (Eugénie's words, 3:441).
Yet to the Chevalier's relatively decent advances
(more normally "proper" than the various acts
Eugénie has just avidly perpetrated), she replies, sin-
cerely injured: "Oh! truly, this is outrageous; you're
taking advantage of my youth to a degree . . . but for
whom is the gentlemen going to take me?" (3:443).
She is defending her honor and her name: "Who
does this gentleman think I am? He is taking me for
someone else, violating my identity." Eugénie (Justine) absorbs each man yet is not altered. She pre-

sents to each new educator-violator a fresh surface to be inscribed.

Likewise, Justine never gives up trying to argue with her consistently incorrigible tormentors, never tires of responding to their harangues. And although Eugénie has been constantly told the general rule that there is no crime, that no act is criminal, upon the explanation of each new specific act she asks whether *this one* is a crime. She provides the perfect foil for a discourse which takes pleasure in defending each crime in great detail, despite the fact that crime in general has been preliminarily negated. Justine never learns her lesson, always remaining in the "delicious state of a rough draft," always inciting the urge to "teach her a lesson," to violate her innocence; Eugénie cannot be taught the very same lessons often enough. Justine never ceases to be scandalized by the predictable transgressions; Eugénie never becomes bored by the repetitive philosophizing.

Immediately after the extremely long pamphlet inserted into *La Philosophie* is read, Dolmancé comments: "It is quite certain that my thinking contains part of these reflections and my words, that have proved it to you, even give to the reading we just did the appearance of a repetition . . ." Eugénie cuts him off in mid-sentence, interrupting in order to declare, "I didn't notice; one cannot say good things too often: however I find some of these principles a bit dangerous" (3:524). Not only does Eugénie not notice repetition (the possibility of becoming jaded eludes her— "one cannot say good things too often"), but her reconstituting naiveté ("however I find *some* of these principles *a bit* dangerous" [my italics]) provides Dolmancé with an excuse for yet another repetition. He must once again explain away her doubts.

Eugénie is the ideal catalyst for the repetition necessary to Klossowski's "ascesis of apathy." Klossowski, in the "Philosophe scélérat," sets the problem up in terms of consistency and inconsistency. Inconsistency is Evil "according to the principle of identity which springs from individuation" (*SMP*67, p. 43). Therefore inconsistency is desirable to the forces of transgression. However, since inconsistency only manifests itself in relation to consistency, as a rupture of that consistency—an intolerable dependency—the goal of the ascesis is the acquisition of "*constancy* in inconsistency. In a word, Sade tried to transgress the very act of outrage [itself the violation of consistency by the momentary inconsistency] by a permanent state of perpetual movement—the movement that much later Nietzsche called: the *innocence of becoming*" (*SMP*67, p. 44). Eugénie, partaking of Juliette's consistent infidelity and Justine's perverse consistency, actualizes "the innocence of becoming," the apotheosis of Sadian outrage, freeing the bud from its teleological subordination to the blossom. "But Sade did no more than glimpse for an instant this transgression of transgression by itself" (*SMP*67, p. 44). The eager virgin is but a moment, a delicious instant of unlimited potential before that potential is actualized, divided into Justine's frigid virginity or Juliette's predictable enthusiasm.

Sade's production contains another version of the virgin-as-whore: Léonore, Aline's sister in *Aline et Valcour*. Whereas Aline (like Justine) is stubbornly virtuous and unwilling to compromise, Léonore (somewhere between Justine and Juliette) is ever willing to pretend compliancy and to use any ruse available to protect her "virtue." Manipulative adventuress Léonore avoids penetration; yet her many exploits share the repetitive predictability of Justine and Juliette. Her equivocation is always in the service of the absolute value: entry to her vagina. The virgin as whore can only be successful with the client who has never seen her operate before, who does not know how the story will end. Her narrated exploits cannot convey the excitement, suspense, and uncertainty of "the innocence of becoming." Within her story, Lénore is as seductive a little tantalizer as Eugénie, constantly getting men and women to compromise their position for her, just as Eugénie provokes Dolmancé to betray his identity as bugger. But Léonore does not excite the reader in the same way, because the reader knows her tease as tease. Eugénie, unlike Léonore, Justine, or Juliette, never tells her own story, never gives away any attempt at mastery in her titillatingly uncertain status. Not set into a structure of narration (*La Philosophie* is a philosophical dialogue), the moment that is Eugénie is neither drawn out into a predictable stasis, nor subordinated to the teleology of a progression towards an end.

Eugénie, the virgin as whore, finds her specular image in the whore as virgin, simulacral commonplace of libertine science. Mme de Saint-Ange instructs her protégée: "There are secrets that mend all these breaches. I promise to make them known to you, and then, should you have fucked like Antoinette, I take upon myself to make you as much a virgin as the day you came into the world" (3:406). Juliette, upon her entry into a brothel, sells her virginity—repeatedly. "In four months, the merchandise is sold to nearly a hundred persons in succession. . . . Each time, Duvergier narrows, readjusts, and for four months it is always the first-fruits that the rascal offers to the public" (*Justine*, 3:62). The secret of innocence is encompassed within the domain of criminal knowledge. Virtue is the property of vice.

Virginity is entangled in the dance of the whore, just another mask in the wanton carnival. Upon apprehension of Augustin's enormous penis along with Saint-Ange's claim of availing herself of that member, vaginally and anally, every night, Dolmancé, whorish counterfeiter *par excellence*, exclaims: "Ah! holy God! what libertinage. . . . Well now, on my honor, I don't know if I could endure it." To which his friend and admirer Saint-Ange replies, "Don't play tight, Dolmancé" (3:452). Virginity, lack of experience, of knowledge, is perverted into a mere playacting, a coy simulation of tightness. If the only reliable way of authenticating a claim to virginity, of distinguishing the coquette from the true virgin, is a physical verification of the orifice's tightness, then the knowledgeable artifices of Duvergier and Saint-Ange make any authentication unreliable. Truth cannot be extricated from the possibility of artifice; virginity is always implicated in the play of coquetry, complicitous falsity, whoring among friends.

The tantalizing moment when the outrageous hussy begins to betray a dependable fidelity to her identity as slut meets the instant of uncertainty when the virgin's persistent resistance just might be an artful come-on. Neither virgin nor whore, but the seductive possibility of metamorphosis of one into the other, disarms and captures the client, the teacher, the reader. The merest hint of inconsistency or complicity, the roughest sketch of infidelity, sets in motion a shake, not yet schematized into foreseeable dance steps: "the innocence of becoming."

Conclusion

Sade: the name screams sex and violence—but community? Bataille's Sade, solitary figure, sovereign without reserve, is too rigid even in his complete profligacy to ever warm to the good humor, exquisite manners, and sparkling companionship of libertine brotherhood. Blanchot puzzles over the coexistence of community with violence: "The relations between these peerless men are rather equivocal." But Blanchot's gesture is to dismiss the moment for the process (be it dialectical or incessant repetition). Only with the felicitous conjuncture of Blanchot and Bataille or Klossowski and Bataille can we approach the reckless friendship of intersexion (graphic mutual cutting).

Bataille's dream of Sade is too pure because it leaves out the friends. Yet Bataille's friends offer us the most exciting stimulus for a reading of Sade, not in their

113

articles on Sade, but on Bataille. Blanchot in "Le Jeu
de la pensée" and "L'Amitié" (his two homages to
Bataille) writes of that which is here with us yet
tauntingly, impossibly out of reach. This (my notion
of the friend as whore) is the counter-generality implicit in the generality: the monstrous yet inseparable
amalgam of the most tame with the most frighten-
ingly inconceivable. Blanchot—when he writes of
Sade—retains too much admiration for Sade's wild-
ness, making Sade unique enough that Bataille's
"normal man" might be able to dismiss the entire
threat as alien and external. It is in the pieces on
Bataille that Blanchot conveys the horrifying yet familiar (horrifying because familiar) coexistence of
unspeakable passions and safe, intimate situations.

Likewise, our reading of Sade is more in keeping
with "Le Corps du néant" and "A propos du simulacre dans la communication de Georges Bataille"
(both pieces, Klossowski-on-Bataille) than with any
of Klossowski's writings "on Sade." From "A propos
du simulacre" comes not only the simulacrum with
its attendant complicity, but the evanescent sovereign moments: at once glorious possibilities and yet
doomed to recuperation into rigid identities. That
glimmer of insubordination (Eugénie as virgin about
to metamorphize into whore, Juliette as whore betraying traces of unsuspected constancy) is romanticized in Klossowski-on-Sade into a too well-pro-
grammed ascesis, too predictable, too foreseeable
in its steps.

Sacking Klossowski's garbage, retrieving "Le
Corps du néant" from its relegation to the trash bin,
yields pungent surprises. Klossowski is unwittingly
swayed by Bataille into compromising his upstanding Christian position. The familiar Bataille proves a

more insidious threat than the alien Sade. Klossowski criticizes Bataille's belief in a "sacred community, universal but secret" (SMP47, p. 168). Yet
this underground conspiracy later appears as the plot
Klossowski declares to be the "constructive" side of
Nietzsche (see "Circulosus Vitiosus," *Nietzsche aujourd'hui?*[1] [Paris: Union Générale, 10 / 18, 1973]).
Unlike a static, temporally and spatially continuous
and containable, secret society (which Blanchot finds
in Sade, but dismisses as a commonplace of Sade's
era), Bataille's conspiracy is a network of monumen-
tal brilliance scattered throughout history: "Sade,
Lautréamont, Hegel, Baudelaire, Rimbaud, Nietzsche,
thus were named some of these *authentic existences
for themselves inasmuch as all of them would con-
verge towards the formation of this order that would
have as its mission to evoke from the heart of the
profane world, that is, the world of functional servil-
ity, the sacred world of the totality of being*" (SMP47,
p. 168).

Such is the Sadian libertine fraternity: underground, not by having a firm foundation in a stable
earth, but by being insidious, underhanded, and
sneaky. And such is the textual network Bataille-
Blanchot-Klossowski: Sadian brothers? sisters?—
counterfeit whores. Moments of conjunction which
ephemerally release Sade's stink from the sterilizing,
rigidifying tomb of literary history. The Sade cele-
brated in the preceding pages finds itself in terrify-
ingly close resemblance to Denis Hollier's awesome,
stunning Bataille (see *La Prise de la concorde* [Paris:
Gallimard, 1974]). "My Sade" (I am at once ashamed
and gratified to say) is neither "mine" nor even
"Sade": mistaken or assumed identity (stolen from
Bataille?). Tangled not only in the net Bataille-Blan-

chot-Klossowski, but that network itself caught in the web Derrida-Lacan-Barthes, and "my" but an inextricable jumble of those networks and others, not the least of which a familiar, personal conspiracy of teachers / readers / friends.

Notes

INTRODUCTION

1. Besides the four major characters, this book includes several minor characters—Guillaume Apollinaire, Roland Barthes, Georg Wilhelm Friedrich Hegel, Alexandre Kojève, Gilbert Lély, Friedrich Nietzsche, Aimé Patri, and André Pieyre de Mandiargues—whose function is merely to articulate and put into relief the relations between the four principals.

2. A recent example can be found on p. 198 of Michel Foucault's *La Volonté de savoir,* vol. 1 of *Histoire de la sexualité:* "Nothing can prevent that thinking the order of the sexual according to the agency of law, death, and sovereignty—whatever might be the references to Sade and Bataille—is not finally a historical 'retroversion.' " (All translations are mine unless otherwise noted.)

CHAPTER 1

1. All quotations from Sade refer to the *Oeuvres complètes du Marquis de Sade,* 16 vols. (Paris: Cercle du Livre précieux, 1967).

2. See the discussion below, chapter 3, pp. 68–71.

3. *Le plaisir du texte*, p. 50.

4. "Sade et l'homme normal" in *L'Erotisme*, p. 209 (hereafter cited as "Homme normal").

5. "Le Secret de Sade," *Critique*, nos. 15–16 (August–September 1947), p. 152 (hereafter cited as "Secret").

6. Guillaume Apollinaire, *L'Oeuvre de Sade*, pp. 14–15.

7. Gilbert Lély, *La Vie du marquis de Sade*, 2:659 (hereafter cited as *Vie de Sade*).

8. "Le Secret de Sade (II)," *Critique*, no. 17 (October 1947), p. 312 (hereafter cited as "Secret II").

9. "L'Homme Souverain de Sade," in *L'Erotisme*, p. 193 (hereafter cited as "Homme souverain").

10. Following a traditional scheme of the nobility's power alliances, the bishop need not marry because he is the duke's brother.

11. "Le Bonheur, l'érotisme et la littérature," *Critique*, no. 36 (May 1949), p. 407 (hereafter cited as "Bonheur").

12. See in particular Bataille's analysis of the *potlatch* in "La Notion du dépense," in *La Part maudite*, pp. 30–35.

13. For an excellent discussion of the relation of Bataille's text to Hegel's, see Jacques Derrida, "De l'économie restreinte à l'économie générale," in *L'Ecriture et la différence*, pp. 369–408.

14. See for example Juliette's murder of Mme de Donis (9:55–62) and Juliette's and Clairwil's murder of Olympe Borghese (9:413–17).

15. See note 14 and also Juliette's murder of Clairwil (9:426–33).

16. "Homme souverain," p. 194, taken from Maurice Blanchot, *Lautréamont et Sade* (Paris: Minuit, 1949), pp. 236–37.

17. "She will be compensated . . . for the trouble she took to . . . procure pleasure" (13:345). See also 13:55: "As regards the errors committed by the storytellers, they will be punished half as much as those of the children because their talent is of service and talents must always

be respected."

18. For examples of the friends' surprising fidelity to their word, see 13:365, 424.

19. See "Homme souverain," p. 186: "[Sade's thought] neglects the factual structure of each real man, which would not be conceivable if we isolated him from the ties that others establish with him, that he himself establishes with others."

20. See "Secret," p. 152: "No one has the right to wish and hope clearly for what Sade obscurely demanded and obtained."

21. See "Homme normal," p. 208: "Thus they are unfaithful to the profound silence that belongs to violence, which never says it exists, and never affirms a right to exist; which always exists without saying it."

22. See "Homme souverain," p. 194, and "Bonheur," p. 409.

23. "Vue d'ensemble: Sade 1740–1814," Critique, no. 78 (November 1953), p. 989.

24. L'Affaire Sade, p. 56.

25. 8:494. For a similar construction of the relation of disgust to desire see the first of Freud's Three Essays on the Theory of Sexuality.

26. Le Petit Robert (Paris: Société du Nouveau Littré, 1970).

27. For a similar discussion on the perversity of innocence, see Jeffrey Mehlman, "How to Read Freud on Jokes: The Critic as Schadchen," New Literary History, (Winter 1975): 439–61 (especially pp. 440–48).

CHAPTER 2

1. Roland Barthes, Barthes par lui-même, p. 63.

2. Maurice Blanchot, "Quelques remarques sur Sade," Critique, nos. 3–4 (August–September 1946), p. 244 (hereafter cited as "Remarques").

3. Blanchot, "La Raison de Sade," in Lautréamont et Sade (hereafter cited as L&S).

4. Georg Wilhelm Friedrich Hegel, *The Phenomenology of Mind*, (hereafter cited as *Phen.*).

5. "Glory" for Bataille is solar "expenditure without reserve," that which is not *propre*, not appropriable, not identical to itself. See "La Notion du dépense" in *La Part maudite*, pp. 23–54.

6. Blanchot, "L'Amitié" in *L'Amitié*, pp. 328–29.

7. Blanchot, "Le Jeu de la penseé," *Critique*, nos. 195–196 (August–September 1963), p. 735.

8. Friedrich Nietzsche, *Thus Spake Zarathustra*, pp. 63–64.

9. *New Cassell's French Dictionary* (New York: Funk & Wagnalls, 1962), p. 598.

10. Of death in its major mode, Blanchot writes: "It never constitutes an event that happens, even when it unexpectedly befalls, never a reality capable of being grasped" (*L'Amitié*, p. 327).

11. Blanchot, *L'Espace littéraire*, p. 348.

12. Hegel's German word "Aufhebung" is retained because of its untranslatable double meaning. "Canceling, superseding, brings out and lays bare its true twofold meaning which we found contained in the negative: to supersede *(aufheben)* is at once to negate and preserve" (Hegel, *Phen.*, pp. 163–64).

13. Alexandre Kojève, *Introduction à la lecture de Hegel*, p. 21.

14. *Vie de Sade*, 2:333.

15. Blanchot, "L'Expérience-limite: L'insurrection, la folie d'écrire," in *L'Entretien infini*, p. 326 (hereafter cited as *L'Entretien*).

16. I am indebted to J. Mehlman for the construction of this fortuitous pun.

17. *Les Infortunes de la vertu* and *Justine ou les malheurs de la vertu*—vols. 2 and 3 of the *Oeuvres complètes*.

18. For further discussion of the *historiennes* in *120 Journées*, see pp. 22–23 of chapter 1 above.

19. No mention is made in this discussion of the function of money because Juliette as whore in-the-major-mode does not recover her desire for absolute prostitution of self through the mask of utility (the need to humiliate oneself, to subjugate oneself in order to earn a living). Just as Sade constantly distinguishes between those who steal for pleasure and those who steal because they need the money; so we locate Juliette's major impropriety in her desire to be whore ("the only sensual pleasure I know is that of satisfying all their deviations"). Only a "real whore" would *want to be a whore.*

20. Justine's narration is Juliette's idea (wish); Juliette's narration is likewise Juliette's (that is, her own) idea.

21. For example, see *Justine*, 3:161–62 (Severino hearing her confession), and 3:232 (Gernande listening to her story).

22. "There wasn't a single one of the sad victims of that establishment who wouldn't have preferred any punishment whatever to the horrible necessity of satisfying the vile pleasures of this debauchee who, being very tedious in the details, often bored them more than he wore them out" (*Nouvelle Justine*, 6:313–14).

CHAPTER 3

1. Georges Bataille, "Le Secret de Sade," *Critique*, nos. 15–16 (August–September 1947), and no. 17 (October 1947), pp. 148–60 and 304–12.

2. Pierre Klossowski, *Sade mon prochain* (Paris: Seuil, 1947) (hereafter cited as *SMP47*.) *SMP47* consists of five studies and three appendices: (1) "Esquisse du système de Sade"—originally published as "Le Mal et la négation d'autrui dans l'oeuvre de D. A. F. de Sade," *Recherches Philosophiques* (1934–35); (2) "Sade et la révolution"—originally a lecture at the Collège de Sociologie (February 1939); (3) "Sous le masque de l'athéisme"—part of which was originally published as "La Monstruosité intégrale," *Acéphale* (June 1936); (4) "La Tenta-

tion du possible"—originally published as "Don Juan selon Kierkegaard," *Acéphale* (July 1937); (5) "Le Corps du néant"—originally a lecture at the Dominican convent of Saint-Maximin, 1941. The second appendix consists of fragments from "Eléments d'une étude psychanalytique sur le Marquis de Sade," *Revue Française de Psychanalyse* 6, nos. 3–4 (1933). A new edition of *Sade mon prochain* was published in 1967 with the same editors. *SMP*67 contains an introduction (explaining its relation to the 1947 edition), the same three appendices, and four studies: (1) "Le Philosophe scélérat"—originally a lecture sponsored by *Tel Quel* (12 May 1966) and appearing in *Tel Quel*, no. 28 (Winter 1967); (2) "L'Esquisse du système de Sade"— the fifth (final) chapter of which is completely changed (except for the first paragraph) from the 1947 version, while the other four chapters are practically untouched (this version first appears as preface to the Cercle du Livre précieux edition of *120 Journées* and is translated as "A Destructive Philosophy" in *Yale French Studies* 35 [December 1965]; (3) "Sade et la révolution"—amended by a long footnote added to chapter five which first appeared as the article "Justine et Juliette" in *Dictionnaire des Oeuvres*, Laffont-Bompiani; and (4) "Sous le masque de l'athéisme"—unchanged. The second appendix ("Eléments d'une étude psychanalytique") is slightly altered.

    3. Aimé Patri, "Notre frère damné," *L'Arche*, no. 26 (June 1947), p. 156.

    4. Klossowski, "De l'opportunité à étudier l'oeuvre du marquis de Sade," *Cahier du Sud*, no. 285 (1947), p. 717.

    5. *L'Arc*, no. 43 (1970), p. 89.

    6. Friedrich Nietzsche, *The Gay Science*, 4:225–26.

    7. Sade, *L'Epoux complaisant et autres recits*.

    8. J. Derrida's discussion of the sponge in his reading of Francis Ponge stimulated this elaboration of a radical notion of the whore.

    9. Friedrich Nietzsche, *Also Sprach Zarathustra*, Erster Teil, "Von Alten und Jungen Weiblein."

10. "Eléments d'une étude psychanalytique sur le Marquis de Sade," pp. 458–74.

11. "The presence of these works of imagination [the novels of the 1950s] *necessarily produces a reaction on the conceptual plane* and permits the expression of *Le Philosophe scélérat* and *Le Cercle vicieux*—which changes and reverses from one end to the other the perspective of what is thought, felt, and said; and deprives of any interest, even nullifies, the false perspective of a bibliography" (Klossowski in *L'Arc*, no. 43 [1970], p. 89—the bibliography).

12. Sade, *Aline et Valcour*, vol. 9 of *Oeuvres complètes* (Paris: Pauvert, 1963), préface de Pierre Klossowski, p. xvii.

13. *Webster's Seventh New Collegiate Dictionary* (Springfield, Mass.: G. & C. Merriam Co., 1967), p. 372.

14. Klossowski, "A propos du simulacre dans la communication de Georges Bataille" *Critique*, nos. 195–196 (August–September 1963), p. 742.

15. *American Heritage Dictionary of the English Language* (New York: American Heritage, 1969), p. 1227.

16. *Webster's Seventh*, p. 829.

17. The rewriting first appears when the "Esquisse" serves as preface to the Cercle du Livre précieux edition of *120 Journées*.

18. For an extended discussion of the Justine / Juliette narration relation, see chapter 2 above, pp. 53–65.

19. *Histoire de Juliette*, vol. 19 of *Oeuvres complètes* (Paris: Pauvert, 1968), p. xxiii.

List of Works Cited

L'Affaire Sade. Paris: Pauvert, 1957.

Apollinaire, Guillaume. *L'Oeuvre de Sade*. Paris: Bibliothèque des curieux, 1909.

L'Arc, no. 43 (1970). Issue devoted to Pierre Klossowski.

Barthes, Roland. *Barthes par lui-même*. Paris: Seuil, 1975.

———. *Le Plaisir du texte*. Paris: Seuil, 1973.

Bataille, Georges. "Le Bonheur, l'érotisme et la littérature." *Critique*, nos. 35 and 36 (1949), pp. 291–306 and 401–11.

———. *L'Erotisme*. Paris: Union Générale, Collection 10 / 18, 1965.

———. *La Part maudite*. Paris: Minuit, Collection Points, 1967.

———. "Le Secret de Sade." *Critique*, nos. 15–16 and no. 17 (1947), pp. 148–60 and 304–12.

———. "Vue d'ensemble: Sade 1740–1814." *Critique*, no. 78 (1953), pp. 989–96.

Blanchot, Maurice. *L'Amitié*. Paris: Gallimard, 1971.

———. *L'Entretien infini*. Paris: Gallimard, 1969.

———. *L'Espace littéraire*. Paris: Gallimard, Collection Idées, 1955.

———. "Le Jeu de la pensée." *Critique,* nos. 195–196 (1963), pp. 734–41.

———. *Lautréamont et Sade.* Paris: Minuit, 1963.

———. "Quelques remarques sur Sade." *Critique,* nos. 3–4 (1946), pp. 239–49.

Derrida, Jacques. *L'Ecriture et la différence.* Paris: Seuil, 1967.

Foucault, Michel. *La Volonté de savoir.* Vol. 1 of *Histoire de la Sexualité.* Paris: Gallimard, 1976.

Freud, Sigmund. *Three Essays on the Theory of Sexuality.* Vol. 7 of *The Complete Psychological Works.* Standard Edition. London: Hogarth Press, 1953.

Hegel, Georg Wilhelm Friedrich. *The Phenomenology of Mind.* Translated by J. B. Baillie. New York: Harper and Row, 1967.

Hollier, Denis. *La Prise de la concorde.* Paris: Gallimard, 1974.

Klossowski, Pierre. "A propos du simulacre dans la communication de Georges Bataille." *Critique,* nos. 195–196 (1963), pp. 742–50.

———. "De l'opportunité à étudier l'oeuvre du marquis de Sade." *Cahiers du Sud,* no. 285 (1947), pp. 717–20.

———. "Eléments d'une étude psychanalytique sur le Marquis de Sade." *Revue Française de Psychanalyse* 6 (1933): 458–74.

———. *Sade mon prochain.* Paris: Seuil, 1947 and 1967.

Kojève, Alexandre. *Introduction à la lecture de Hegel.* Paris: Gallimard, 1947.

Lély, Gilbert. *La Vie du marquis de Sade.* 2 vols. Paris: Gallimard, 1952 and 1957.

Mehlman, Jeffrey. "How to Read Freud on Jokes: The Critic as *Schadchen.*" *New Literary History* 6 (1975): 439–61.

Nietzsche aujourd'hui? Vol. I: *Intensités.* Paris: Union Générale, Collection 10 / 18, 1973.

Nietzsche, Friedrich. *Thus Spake Zarathustra.* Translated by Thomas Common. New York: Modern Library, 1917.

————. *The Gay Science.* Translated by Walter Kaufmann. New York: Vintage, 1974.

Patri, Aimé. "Notre frère damné." *L'Arche,* no. 26 (1947), 152–57.

Sade, Donatien Alphonse François, marquis de. *Oeuvres complètes.* 16 vols. Paris: Cercle du Livre précieux, 1967.

————. *Aline et Valcour.* Vols. 9–12 of *Oeuvres complètes.* Paris: Pauvert, 1963.

————. *L'Epoux complaisant et autres récits.* Paris: Union Générale, Collection 10 / 18, 1968.

————. *Histoire de Juliette ou les prospérités du vice.* Vols. 19–24 of *Oeuvres complètes.* Paris: Pauvert, 1968.

Appendix

CROSS-REFERENCES TO ENGLISH EDITIONS OF SADE

For those who wish to use the Grove Press English translations of Sade's works, I am providing this quick page reference. The first column refers to the page of this book on which the quotation is found; the second column is the reference to the Cercle du livre précieux *Oeuvres complètes* as found in this text; the third column refers to the Grove Press edition when one exists.

Grove Editions:
1. *Justine, Philosophy in the Bedroom, and Other Writings* (1966)
2. *The 120 Days of Sodom and Other Writings* (1967)
3. *Juliette* (1968)
NA. Not Available

Gallop page	OC reference	Grove reference
11	8:209	3:217–18
15	13:2–3	2:192
	13:4	2:194

16	13:364	2:592
17	13:384	2:618
	13:60	2:252–53
18	6:331	NA
19	6:331	NA
20	8:403–4	3:421
	8:406	3:424
	8:403	3:420
	9:18	3:608–9
21	8:560	3:582
22	8:575–76	3:598
	9:217	3:812
	9:312	3:909
	7:100	NA
	13:55	2:246–47
	13:429	2:670
23	13:270–71	2:485
26	9:276–80	3:874–77
32	6:237	NA
33	7:183	NA
	8:403	3:420
35	8:227	3:236
45	9:362	3:959
	13:27	2:218
53	3:83	1:484
54	9:586	3:1193
	9:587	3:1193
56	3:308	1:705–6
57	9:86	3:680
58	9:412	3:1013
61	3:66	1:468
	3:74	1:476
63	3:74	1:476
64	3:271	1:669
	3:193	1:593
67	6:154	NA
72	8:207	3:215
	8:70–71	3:63

75	3:413	1:229
76	14:117	NA
80	3:414	1:230
83	3:431	1:247
84	3:431	1:247
97	9:86	3:680
	3:373	1:188
	3:374	1:189
98	7:165–66	NA
99	3:375	1:191
100	3:545	1:362
	3:546	1:363
101	3:547	1:364
108	3:441	1:257
	3:443	1:259
109	3:524	1:339–40
111	3:406	1:222
	3:62	1:464
112	3:452	1:268
118	9:55–62	3:653–56
	9:413–17	3:1016–18
	9:426–33	3:1027–34
	13:345	2:568–69
	13:55	2:246–47
119	13:365, 424	2:590, —
121	3:161–62	1:562
	3:232	1:630
	6:313–14	NA

Index